FAST YOUNG BEAUTIFUL

A Myth in Two Acts

Ethan Warren

D1522357

ETHAN WARREN

FAST YOUNG BEAUTIFUL premiered at Northern Kentucky University in Highland Heights, KY from April 3 – 14, 2019. The production was directed by Nicole Perrone. The cast was:

DENNIS	Charles Adams
DEAN	Landis Helwig
NATALIE	Rachel Kazee
NICK/STEVENS	Alex Slade
COREY/ROCK	Austin Adams
LIZ/NATALIE'S MOTHER	Sarah Hack
MARY	Katie Tierney
BOBBY	Brayden Glass
REPORTER	Kylie Flick
FIGMENT A	Jerrod Gruber
FIGMENT B	Raven Burns-Gibson
FIGMENT C	Brooke Hardin
FIGMENT D	Tyler Rosenblatt
FIGMENT E	Nick Palazzolo

I would like to acknowledge the contributions of my friend Jackson Ross, who brought to my attention the story's core relationships, and whose suggestions provided the earliest framework for the play's shape and tone.

CAST OF CHARACTERS

DENNIS – age 19; a sincere but impulsive young man, always searching for someone to help him become who he wants to be.

DEAN – in his mid-20s; moody and distant, he uses the legend of his genius to hide from the world and protect himself.

NATALIE – age 16; optimistic and ambitious, eager to grow up as fast as possible.

NICK – in his mid-40s; cocky but insecure, chasing the admiration and approval of those younger than him in search of a second crack at his youth.

COREY – in his mid-20s; conservative and mannered, he's highly trained in his craft and takes it very seriously.

STEVENS – in his mid-50s; authoritative and guarded but capable of warmth, he's haunted by painful memories but living on as best he can.

ROCK – in his mid-30s; an old-fashioned movie star, all bravado and good cheer, but it masks both insecurity and cutthroat ambition.

LIZ – in her mid-20s; an old-fashioned movie star, all glamour and good cheer, but it masks both insecurity and loneliness.

MARY – age 17; a fading child star, cynical and fierce.

BOBBY – age 17; a fading child star, affable but strong.

NATALIE'S MOTHER – in her mid-40s; a stern Russian immigrant.

REPORTER – an eager young woman.

TV HOST – a jolly, unseen male voice.

FIGMENTS A thru E – shifting roles giving the era voice. Gender-neutral.

SETTING

Various locations in Southern California and Texas, 1955.

NOTES

STAGING: Staging should be fairly bare, with expressionist elements to create settings—if possible, film set items such as apple boxes, tripods, and lighting equipment might be appropriate.

COSTUMING: When Dean is not working on a film, he should wear a black turtleneck and glasses. For the entirety of shooting in Act One, whether on set or not, he should wear white T-shirt, blue jeans, and red windbreaker. For the entirety of shooting in Act Two, he should wear tan ranch-hand garb. When he wraps at the end, back to turtleneck and glasses.

DIALOGUE: An ellipsis (…) indicates a character is lost in thought. A dash (–) indicates the character has cut themselves off. A slash (/) indicates one character has been cut off by another, and this is where the following line should begin. At times, dialogue may appear grammatically incorrect. This is a conscious choice in an effort to mimic the cadence of real speech.

CASTING: In a realistic rendering, due to the story's time and place, the principal characters would most likely be white. However, it is the playwright's view that theater allows enough suspension of disbelief that roles should be filled by the best actor available, regardless of ethnicity.

FIGMENT SEQUENCES: Stage directions in these expressionistic sequences are a suggestion meant to convey the rough shape of a tone. Directors should consider themselves free to reinvent the staging on these sequences in keeping with their own vision for the production.

A FEW WORDS ON TRUTH

This is a work of creative nonfiction. The events are drawn from a wide variety of primary and secondary accounts of the events of 1955. Due to the often-contradictory nature of these accounts, changes were made in order to create a cohesive narrative. Due to the often-messy nature of real life, further changes were made in order to create a satisfying narrative. While great pains were taken to not carelessly misrepresent the final months of James Dean's life, there was enough guesswork and invention involved that this should not be viewed as a fully nonfiction account of those months.

While the names of many central characters suggest real people, full names have been deliberately elided. These are *characters* (some of them composites, some of them imagined), and their words and behavior are invented. The playwright hopes that producers will forego seeking impersonators of any known figure, instead seeking emotionally true performances. On a related note, for the films Dean shot in 1955, titles have been omitted and identifying details altered in order to fit the themes of the play and evade any demands of verisimilitude.

Ultimately, this play should be viewed through the lens of *ecstatic truth*, which is said to be poetic, mysterious, and elusive, reachable only through fabrication, imagination, and stylization. We have documentaries to provide unvarnished truth. We go to the theater to dream. And that is what you are invited to do now as you turn the page.

ETHAN WARREN

Being a good actor isn't easy. Being a man is even more difficult. I want to be both before I'm done.

James Dean (allegedly)

ETHAN WARREN

ACT ONE

*Figment A enters and addresses the
audience in solemn reporter's tones.*

FIGMENT A

James Dean is dead at the age of 24. But Hollywood will long
remember this handsome, moody actor who showed more real talent
in his brief career than a trainload of veteran celluloid heroes.

Figment B enters.

FIGMENT B

California Highway Patrol said a car driven by a local college student
turned left off Highway 466 onto Highway 41 and collided head-on
with Dean's Porsche. The student suffered minor injuries.

Figment C enters.

FIGMENT C

One moviegoer in Philadelphia said of Dean, *I felt as though he were
acting the part of all teenagers.*

Figment D enters.

FIGMENT D

James Dean was a promising young actor, but he was traveling at
furious speed. When a motorist's negligence contributes to his end, it
can be reckoned only as a careless suicide.

Figment E enters.

FIGMENT E

His brief career was as bright as a meteor which flows like a golden
tear down the dark cheeks of night. And gifts such as his are not
suddenly wiped out in the wreckage of a car.

FIGMENT B

The ambulance driver said that Dean was still alive when taken from the wreckage but died en route to the hospital.

Dennis enters and walks among the figments, listening and reacting, though they're unaware of him.

FIGMENT E

As long as we remember, the influence of others lives in our hearts.

FIGMENT D

Though one is disposed to speak well of the dead, it is lucky this was not a case of *murder* on the road.

FIGMENT C

The Philadelphia moviegoer went on to say, *I feel the death of James Dean had a purpose for America.*

FIGMENT A

He was a unique star in the Hollywood galaxy. Perhaps he did not belong here.

FIGMENT E

And though we weep for the dead, we must feel that James Dean, who lived so dangerously, would have been pleased his last act came as it did, as last nights must come to all earthly things.

Dennis has grown frustrated.

DENNIS
(into audience)

Hey!

The figments freeze.

DENNIS

Sorry. Force of habit, trying to get attention – so, I wanted to talk a little about him. About James. I thought it would help…sort some stuff out. For all of us.

The figments drift offstage as Dennis talks. He is already struggling to find the words.

DENNIS

I was reading he had a friend in New York. And when he came to Hollywood in '54 to start making movies, he sent a photo. They printed it in a magazine, this photo of him jumping off a train.

Dean enters upstage, partially obscured by shadow.

DENNIS

But he looked – he looked like he was *flying*. And on the back, he wrote to his friend –

DEAN

I bet you'd tell me to be careful, wouldn't you?
(chuckle)

DENNIS

I used to believe in destiny. Like if you were a genius, a genuine genius, then something was protecting you. Like what you had to share with the world was so important, you'd be safe.

Dean lights a cigarette, a flare in the dark.

DENNIS

But I been thinking more and more about the guy in the photo. Frozen in midair. You know he's gonna crash, but you just think – *maybe…*

DEAN

I bet you'd tell me to be safe, wouldn't you? I bet.

He chuckles again and exits.

DENNIS
I don't think I believe in destiny anymore. I don't know what I believe. That's why I wanna tell you about it all. The important stuff. It's already…getting a little hazy. I'll do my best to…recreate it. Might have to fudge some stuff, but hey, that's what makes it a story, right?
(pauses to think)
I guess I'd start the night before the crash. *My* crash, I mean. I know Nick's phone rang real late.

A phone begins to ring. Dennis exits,
and Nick enters, trying to wake up.
He answers the phone.

NICK
Hello?

Silence.

NICK
Gloria? Is it you? Honey, please, you gotta forgive me, it was just/a stupid –

DEAN *(voice)*
Hiya, Nick.

Pause. Nick gets his bearings.

NICK
James?

Dean is affable, but he's keeping
emotion at bay.

DEAN *(voice)*
I been thinking…I'm not gonna do your picture. Sorry.

NICK
Now why in the world/would you –

DEAN *(voice)*
I'm real sorry. I just can't come back.

NICK
Come back from where? James, what's going on?

DEAN *(voice)*
(suddenly very vulnerable)
Do you think I should? Do you think it's worth it?

NICK
I know it'll be worth it for me, it'll *certainly* be worth it for
Warners/so if –

DEAN *(voice)*
OK, well, too bad. Cuz I'm not coming back.

NICK
James, where the hell *are* you? Talk to me! Are you in trouble? You
sound/so –

DEAN *(voice)*
I'll see ya.

The line goes dead.

NICK
Well, *shit*.

*He exits as Dennis enters and sits, a
script rolled up in his hand. He's
anxious but tries to seem cool. He flips
through the script and rolls it back up.*

*Natalie enters. Her bearing is calm
and collected, trying to be mature.
Dennis hops up, offers his hand.*

DENNIS
Hi!

> NATALIE
>
> *(wary)*

Hello.

> DENNIS

Sorry! Natalie, right? I've seen all your pictures, I just forget nobody in this town knows ME yet!

> NATALIE

Oh. Yes, well – hello.

> DENNIS

I'm Dennis. I'm doin' the screen tests with all the girls.

> NATALIE

I'm not going to read with James Dean?

> DENNIS

Oh, nah, I think he's out of town or something.

> NATALIE
>
> *(crestfallen)*

I see.

> DENNIS

Does the big star usually read in screen tests?

> NATALIE

We know each other sort of. We did a TV picture together. I thought…it might help.

> *She deflates, then puffs herself back up.*

> NATALIE

So how is my competition?

> DENNIS

I've read with a LOT of girls…

NATALIE

Has anybody stood out in particular?

DENNIS

It's all a blur. You really want this part, huh?

NATALIE

Everyone in this town thinks of me as a child star. And child stars have a shelf life. I need to…

DENNIS

Grow up?

NATALIE

Playing a juvenile delinquent would certainly change the headline.

DENNIS

Oh. I didn't exactly analyze it, I'm just happy to be working.

NATALIE

You're in this picture?

DENNIS

Yeah, just signed my contract with Warners. This is picture number one. It's a small part/but I'm –

NATALIE

So you roll into town from – where, exactly?

DENNIS

Dodge City, Kansas. Born and raised and then got the/hell out.

NATALIE

And right into a James Dean picture!
(frustrated, sarcastic)
You must be quite the talented individual.

DENNIS

Christ, people are head over heels for that guy! He did ONE picture, already they're/talkin' like –

NATALIE

Did you SEE that one picture?

DENNIS

It was fine.

NATALIE

I'd call it quite a lot better than *fine*.

Nick enters.

NICK

All right, cats, you want to get this show on the road?

NATALIE

(suddenly anxious)

Yes! Absolutely!

She rushes to Nick. Dennis follows.

NATALIE

Thank you SO much for seeing me.

NICK

(slightly put off by her eagerness)

Happy to. That is my job.

DENNIS

She thought she might be reading with James Dean.

NICK

No, James is – he's very busy at the moment, I'm afraid.

NATALIE

I understand. We're friends. Sort of. It really would be SUCH a joy
to/be able –

NICK

Let's slate and begin, shall we?

NICK (cont'd)
(*looks into audience as though speaking
into a camera*)
Judy screen test number 36.

*He claps. Natalie is shocked by the
number.*

NICK
Whenever you're ready.

*Natalie takes a moment, getting into
character. She holds the script, but she's
off-book.*

NATALIE *(in character)*
They won't just forgive and forget, you know.

Dennis reads off the script, slightly rote.

DENNIS *(in character)*
You think this whole mess was my fault? What was I supposed to
do?

NATALIE *(in character)*
It doesn't matter. People like that see what they want to see.

DENNIS *(in character)*
Do you hate me, too?

NATALIE *(in character)*
I don't know what I feel anymore.

DENNIS *(in character)*
(*sigh*)
Shame it all went sideways. This day started out so top-notch.

NATALIE *(in character)*
Why's that?

> DENNIS
> *(half in character, halfway sincere)*

I met you.

> NATALIE *(in character)*
> *(anguished)*

Just being around them makes me hate myself! I wish I could just live for myself! Be/who I –

> NICK

All right, we'll call it a cut there. Thanks a lot, both of you.

> NATALIE

What? No, please! I have/a whole –

> NICK

I've been around the block a few times, I have an intuition. Don't read anything into it.

> *Natalie is dumbstruck.*

> DENNIS

Well, c'mon, if she thinks she's got more in the tank, don't you think/she's earned –

> NICK

Hey, Dennis, I appreciate the input, but what if you tried listening and learning?

> DENNIS

Sure, no disrespect, but she's got experience, she's/got –

> NATALIE
> *(explosive)*

This is ME! I AM this girl! It's not just some PART for me!

> NICK

I'm glad the role had an impact, that always means a lot to a/director.

NATALIE

You're not LISTENING to me!

She tries to rush Nick, but Dennis
grabs her elbow.

DENNIS

C'mon, let's go have a smoke.

NATALIE

I'm not just some kid star! I'm GROWN! I'm WILD!

DENNIS
(to Nick)
You want passion in your actors? Cuz you don't fake this.

Nick plays dismissive, but he heard.
Dennis and Natalie move downstage as
Nick exits.

DENNIS

I might be new in town, but all this *listen and learn* shit – y'know, I been Hamlet, I been/Oedipus–

NATALIE

Thank you. For everything back there. It's nice to not feel alone in one of those rooms.

DENNIS

Well, you certainly made more of an impression than any of the other girls

NATALIE

If I don't get this part…I think it's curtains for me.

DENNIS

I see you in magazines every week, people don't just forget that overnight. And directors know it.

NATALIE

Nothing in those magazines is real. My mother orchestrates it all – I wasn't kidding, you know. When I read that script about a girl with controlling parents who wants to – run as fast as she can and never look back? It's like I was reading my own life.

DENNIS

So do you even like acting? Or is it just your mom?

NATALIE

(sigh)

It's the only way I've ever experienced being *free*. If I quit, I'll be in some kind of cage my whole life.

DENNIS

That's a damn good way of putting it.

NATALIE

But she'd rather I act with nice pinup stars she can parade me around with for photographers. Not someone at risk of making an *interesting* film. Not someone like James Dean.

DENNIS

Well he's a big star, doesn't that make her happy?

NATALIE

Oh, I've acted with stars before. James is…different. Nobody's quite figured him out yet.

DENNIS

Well, you got a mom who cares too much, I got a mom who doesn't give a rat's ass, I don't know who's got it worse.

NATALIE

I think I do.

DENNIS

(laugh)

Yeah, me too, I guess. I was just tryin' to make you feel better.

Natalie cracks a sad smile. Dean enters.

NATALIE

Oh my God, there he is!

DENNIS

Who?

NATALIE

James! Hi!

Dennis does a double-take.

DENNIS

THAT'S James Dean? He looks like a hobo!

Dean glances their way, disinterested.

DEAN

Hi.

NATALIE

It's Natalie, we were in/a television –

DEAN

I remember. Good t'see ya.

Dennis goes to Dean, sticking his hand out.

DENNIS

Hey, I'm Dennis. I'm with Warners, I'm gonna be doin' –

Dean ignores Dennis and exits.

DENNIS

Asshole!

NATALIE

He doesn't behave like us, but that's what makes him *him*.

DENNIS

That's a convenient excuse.

NATALIE

I mean it. On set, he'd sit in the corner doing…rituals, movements, like he was charging a battery.

DENNIS

Oh come on. You learn the lines, listen to the director, do the job. It's worked for a few centuries, hasn't it? What's he think he is, some kinda/genius?

NATALIE

He's a genius.

DENNIS

Well, I'm good, and I'm only one picture behind him. The race is on.

NATALIE
(laugh)
Best of luck. He's the fastest driver around, too. They forbid him from driving during a shoot, they think he'll wreck with a picture half-finished.

Dennis puts a cigarette in his mouth.

DENNIS

Sounds like a peach.
(lights smoke, offers her the pack)
Your mom let you smoke?

NATALIE

I keep mints and perfume for just that reason.

She takes a cigarette and he lights it.

DENNIS

Well, keep your chin up. You were really good in there. I'd bet on you. I'd bet big.

He turns to go.

NATALIE

Are you busy tonight?

He turns back.

DENNIS

I'm alone in the universe, I'm never busy.

NATALIE

I'm meeting some friends at Googie's Diner. Would you want to join?

DENNIS

That could be nice. Where is it?

NATALIE

On Sunset near Runyon. Be there in a few hours. Maybe you could have your way with me later.

She takes a seductive puff and exits.

DENNIS
(muttered)
Holy shit.
(to audience)
Girls don't talk like that in Dodge City, Kansas, obviously. Anyway, I guess around then –

Nick enters, skimming a script.
Dennis exits as Dean enters.

NICK

James! You're – you came back!

Dean goes to the wall and considers.

DEAN

This is really beautiful stuff.

NICK

My office wall?

*Dean makes a barely perceptible face of
disappointment, and then tries again.*

DEAN

Is it real, or a reproduction?

*Nick is confused. Dean tries again
with more force, looking for Nick to
join him in the game.*

DEAN

If it's a reproduction, the technique is exquisite.

NICK

(catching on)
Do you think I'd buy a reproduction? What do you take me for,
some kind of philistine?

Dean nods and turns around.

DEAN

I'm reconsidering.

NICK

Oh, thank Christ! I don't know if they'd let me do it without you.

DEAN

Why do you care so much about this picture?

NICK

Because I want to keep making more of them!

Dean nods. Good answer; not good enough.

DEAN

I need two things.

NICK

Consider it done!

DEAN

I need a closed set. No reporters unless I invite them.

NICK

Easy. This is supposed to be a scrappy little B-picture, Warners won't even notice.
(ironic)
Teenage problems aren't *serious*/you know.

DEAN

I need you to shoot in color. Make it a spectacle, I want that screen soaked and bleeding.

NICK

Well hang on, if we're calling it a *little* movie, I don't know how I ask for/the budget –

DEAN

It's what I need.

NICK

OK. I'll try my best.

DEAN

I didn't say try.

NICK

I'll make it happen.

DEAN

And I need you to promise you'll let me do my work. My way.

NICK

That's why I hired you, isn't it?

DEAN

I'll keep reconsidering.

NICK

James – you sounded so *scared* on the phone. You sounded like/you might –

Dean starts to go, then glances at the wall.

DEAN

I don't know if I believe you. I think that's a reproduction.

He exits. Nick rubs his head and exits, too.

Dennis enters.

DENNIS

I got down to Sunset early, just walked around.

The figments enter, surging around him.

FIGMENT A

(an affable TV host)

The thrill of Los Angeles is in the air! A city which has grown faster than any other in America, and which sees a constant influx of pilgrims from every corner of the world!

FIGMENT C

(an ecstatic poet)

Hollywood, Hollywood, beautiful Hollywood!

DENNIS

And yeah, I had a little liquid courage.

FIGMENT E

Each year, Los Angeles enjoys the presence of thousands of visitors drawn by the magical fascination of the motion picture industry!

FIGMENT C

Bright lights tremendous! Foolish! Stupendous!

> *The figments start to close in on Dennis.*

DENNIS

I don't need to tell you what happens to a guy when he's got a shot with a world-famous beauty.

> *Dennis drinks from a flask as the figments push him along like a wave, moving him forward and back, making slow progress. He's thrilled, a little anxious.*

FIGMENT B

(a cynical gossip)

America's self-righteous scolds malign this colony and all its works, considering Hollywood synonymous with sin.

FIGMENT C

Dramatics are everywhere! Tragedy in the air!

FIGMENT A

Every single industry in Southern California benefits directly from the motion picture business!

FIGMENT D

America's abundant goody-two-shoes have branded Hollywood a new Sodom and Gomorrah.

FIGMENT C

A platinum fortress, stupendous and gorgeous!

FIGMENT E

They call this the miracle mile, and truly, it is exactly that.

FIGMENT B

But while puritanical armies scream for boycott, Americans flock to the cinema by the multitude.

> *The figments drift back revealing*
> *Natalie, Bobby, and Mary sitting at a*
> *booth. The figments exit.*

NATALIE

Dennis! Over here!

> *He goes to her.*

NATALIE

You want a malted?

DENNIS

They got beer?

MARY

She's sixteen.

DENNIS

Oh. Sure, yeah, malted sounds good.

> *Natalie starts to go.*

MARY

A woman never buys a man's drink!

NATALIE

He's my guest. And he's an ingénue.

> *She leaves. Mary glares at Dennis.*

MARY

You tell me right now exactly what your intentions are with that young girl.

Dennis peers at her.

MARY

What?

BOBBY

You're wondering if she's Little Bo Peep, aren't you?

DENNIS

Yes! Wow, that's incredible, I grew up with your voice.

MARY

I asked you a question!

DENNIS
(laughs)
Sorry, it's just a little surreal to get scolded by Bo Peep.

Bobby laughs.

MARY

What's funny?
(to Dennis)
Don't you recognize Little Nemo?

DENNIS
(shocked)
Are you really him?

BOBBY

Guilty.

DENNIS

Man, I didn't know I was coming to a child star meet'n'greet. Hey, how'd they make that bed fly?

BOBBY

It was actually pretty neat. They rigged/it with –

MARY

If you hurt my friend, I will destroy your entire life. Never doubt the fury of a fading child star.

DENNIS

Have I got a reputation already or something?

BOBBY

Mary's, ah…protective. Natalie's not like other girls.

DENNIS

Yeah, no kidding.

MARY

Did she tell you about the gypsy?

DENNIS

She did not.

BOBBY

Natalie's mom grew up in Russia. When she was young, this gypsy read her fortune, and told her two things. One: her daughter would be a famous beauty. Two: her daughter would be cursed.

DENNIS

Well that's insane.

MARY

Don't you *ever* say that to her.

BOBBY

OK, easy, Bo Peep.

Natalie returns with the malted.

NATALIE

Your malted, sire. Pay me back as you see fit.

NATALIE (cont'd)
(sitting down)
Did Dennis tell you he's in the new James Dean picture?

BOBBY
No shit! You meet him yet?

DENNIS
Yeah, he seems like a piece of work.

BOBBY
Nah, guys like him come along once in a generation, maybe less. He's changing the game.

DENNIS
He's made one picture! Why doesn't Kazan get the credit for directing it outta him?

MARY
You don't direct that *out* of someone. The first moment he's onscreen —

BOBBY
And he's not even talking! But he *fills* that screen.

MARY
He fills the theater! There's something radiating off him, he's not acting, he's overflowing.

DENNIS
I've studied acting too. He's good at pretending. It's not like he unlocked some portal to the soul.

MARY
That is exactly what he did.

DENNIS
Well even if he did, that's not a license to treat people like shit.

NATALIE

He's been through a lot. You know he's an orphan?

BOBBY

No, he had a dad, his dad just sold him off when he was little.

DENNIS

What?

MARY

He had to run away and ride the rails in a train car full of coffins just to get to California.

NATALIE

They say he sleeps on razors.

BOBBY

You hear he beat the piss out of Brando?

MARY

Did you hear he and Vampira do Satantic rituals to make him a better actor?

NATALIE

Really?

MARY

That's what I heard!

DENNIS

He's a guy with a job! It's a good job, but isn't this an industry town?

BOBBY

Look, let me tell you something. When my dad was in Korea, fighting in the mud for no good reason – it almost broke him. But what he always talks about is – the movies. They got the reels shipped, they'd hunker down, and the confusion would just…disappear. This business you two are in, you give people that gift. And the world's only getting more confusing. So take it serious.

DENNIS

Just me and Natalie? What about you?

BOBBY

I'm last year's model. Nobody wants to see Little Nemo with acne.

NATALIE

I hope that's not true.

BOBBY

It's different for girls.

MARY

Well bless you for believing in it. I'm exhausted. There's some sick
people in this town.

NATALIE

You sound so cynical!

MARY

Not by choice.
        (standing)
I'm tired, let's get going.

NATALIE

I think I'll stay out a while longer. I told Dennis I'd show him the
town.

MARY

I thought we could go back/to my –

DENNIS

Oh, yeah, I'd love to check out the sights.

> *Mary and Natalie exchange looks.*
> *Mary relents.*

MARY
        (glaring at Dennis)
I see you.

ETHAN WARREN

> *Mary and Bobby exit. Natalie turns to Dennis, smiles, and sidles up next to him.*

DENNIS
(to audience)
So we went for a drive. And I bought us a bottle. And we drank the bottle.

> *Dennis and Natalie stand, taking their drive.*

DENNIS
And we drove up into the hills to see the lights down below. And she told me —

NATALIE
I'm cursed, y'know.

DENNIS
And she told me —

> *She snuggles close to him.*

NATALIE
I don't feel safe anywhere in this world. But I feel safe with you.

DENNIS
I was soaring. We parked, we had a pretty good time. She said I made her *safe*. I was *soaring*.

> *Natalie drifts offstage. Dennis stands*

DENNIS
We got back on the road. Then I WAS soaring. Then there was glass everywhere.

> *As he speaks, he becomes drunk and traumatized.*

DENNIS

And then we were at the hospital. And –

A phone rings.

DENNIS

(talking on phone)

Nick! It's Dennis, we're at Mount Sinai – it's all my fault! – Natalie said to call! We had a head-on smash, we flipped, and it's *my fault!*

> *The line goes dead. Dennis hugs his arms and paces. Nick rushes on. Dennis looks up and tries to speak, but Nick grabs him by the arm, and slaps his face.*

DENNIS

I didn't –

NICK

You shut the hell up! And you STRAIGHTEN the hell up!

DENNIS

She said to call you! I thought it was a good idea! I thought you knew what it was like/to be us!

NICK

Where is she?

DENNIS

In there. She won't let her mom in until she sees you.

NICK

Why?

> *Dennis shrugs. A nurse pushes Natalie on in a wheelchair.*

                    NICK
            (tender)
Hey, kid.

            Natalie lunges, wild and thrilled.

                    NATALIE
Kid? No!
            (grabbing his shirt)
The cops, the doctors, all of them – they called me a juvenile
delinquent!

                    NICK
What?

                    NATALIE
They all said it! A real live juvenile delinquent! So? Do I have the
part?

            Nick pulls away from Natalie.

                    NICK
Just rest, darling.

            He turns on Dennis, threatening.

                    NICK
No more bullshit from you. That's our leading lady. We need her in
one piece.

            *He squeezes Natalie's hand, then
            exits.*

                    NATALIE
We did it!

                    DENNIS
I didn't keep you safe. I'm so sorry.

NATALIE

Dennis! You saved me!

She laughs as she's wheeled off. Dennis
shifts into another scene, calling home.

DENNIS

Hey, Ma…yeah, it's Dennis! Christ!…Hey, tomorrow's the big day, starting my first picture…No, but you know who IS starring? James Dean!…He's a big deal! They say he's gonna be bigger than Brando!…You know who Brando is, Ma, don't – …well Dean's one of the biggest stars out here, and I'll be onscreen with him…Look, it's pretty unusual for someone to get a contract this quick. I only – …I'm not begging! Say you're proud of me if you want, I'm not – …Hey! What if I told you I had a girlfriend? A pretty damn famous one!…Because I thought you might be happy! I'm chasing my dreams, and I'm catching 'em!…Hey! I said HEY! If you're not gonna be happy for me no matter WHAT - …I'm not being difficult! Stop YELLING…I SAID if you're not gonna be – hello?

The line is dead.

DENNIS
(muttered)

If you're not gonna be happy, how about you be sorry? Huh? How about that?

Nick enters, sits upstage, flipping
through his script.

DENNIS
(to audience)

Anyway. We went to a meeting. Nick had a bungalow at the Chateau Marmont. His marriage was on the rocks. When there were lines in contracts about how stars behaved, the Marmont's where they misbehaved. When the world thought Harlow was on her honeymoon, she was there gettin' busy with Gable. Errol Flynn brought girls there, and let's just say they were *girls*. If you're in Hollywood, and you want to get into trouble without gettin' in trouble – well, that's where Nick was living.

Natalie enters and goes to him.

NATALIE

What's cookin', good lookin'?

Corey enters, too.

DENNIS

Hey. Wanna get into a little trouble after this?

Natalie plays with his fingers.

NATALIE

Oh, I think I could get my head around that idea.

DENNIS

How long's a read-through usually take?

NATALIE

About as long as the picture runs, but I don't believe Nick intends to
do things the typical way.

COREY

I believe you're correct.

Dennis and Natalie look.

COREY

Pardon. Nice to meet you, they call me Corey.

DENNIS

Should I?

COREY

If you'd like. My real name's a bit more semitic. It was suggested I
might want something –

DENNIS

Anti-semitic?

Natalie smacks his arm, reproachful.

COREY

If you want to talk about unusual, my audition was thirty actors running up and down a bleacher.

NATALIE

Really? Why?

COREY

Well, I'm the gang leader –

NATALIE

Oh, you're my boyfriend!

COREY

Charmed, I'm sure. When I got the call I thought, I'm a bit old, but I'm a professional, I can try. They sent me to a high school gym with thirty little…whippersnappers. Nick told us to run to the top of the bleachers and back as fast as we could. The others started *racing*, but I don't like to sweat. I walked up to the top, turned around to see Nick smirking at me, and I knew I'd gotten it.

NATALIE

What a vision!

DENNIS

What about trusting your director?

NATALIE

He needs to get the best work out of us!

DENNIS
(very anxious)
I don't respond so good to games.

NATALIE

This is going to be such an honor. I can't believe it.

Dennis looks to Corey, who shrugs—
We'll see. *Nick stands up.*

NICK

All right, cats, shall we begin?

Natalie rushes to him. Dennis goes,
apprehensive.

DENNIS

Hey, Nick, I wanted to make sure – my part's not so big, but all my lines are gonna stay in/right?

NICK

Later, Dennis, but I'm very interested.

He shakes Corey's hand. Then
Natalie's, tenderly.

COREY

Is James Dean coming?

NICK

Not tonight. He'll be here when we need him.

DENNIS

Guy's getting paid probably ten times what we are, and he can't come to the table read?

Natalie shushes him, Nick ignores
him.

NICK

All right, then. The truth is this: acting is to be *experienced*, not *directed*. My role is to facilitate that. I don't mean to be your boss.

He looks around, relishing their
interest.

NICK

Nobody hates youth as much as the young. Nobody takes you seriously, so you want to grow up and have your feelings valued. I say we make a picture that FORCES people to value your feelings.

Natalie nods, enraptured.

NICK

Films imitate life, but there's never been one that *captures* it. A camera's a magical thing, and nobody's harnessed that power. If we do so, I believe we could start a revolution in this country.

Corey scoffs involuntarily.

NICK

I was part of one before, y'know. In the arts wing of the New Deal, we made protest theater, *revolution* theater. We showed the pain America was feeling, the way the government was crushing America under its boot. We scared people, they called us commies, but *we* had the power. We changed things. That's what I want to do again, and this time, I want to bring you along.

He holds out his hands, waiting for a
response. Natalie murmurs her
agreement.

NICK

I want you to be my family, and I want to be yours. So I want you to spend the night together tonight, and tomorrow night. Go to the beach and howl at the moon, go climb to the roof of an abandoned warehouse. Get to know yourselves, get to know each other.

DENNIS

(anxious)
What about the read-through?

NICK

Read-throughs are for squares. We're revolutionaries. Meanwhile, I'd like to have conferences one-on-one to get your perspectives. Natalie, could you stay a while? Help me get to know Judy better?

NATALIE

Really? Of course!

Nick holds out a hand, inviting. They exit.

COREY
(laughs, claps Dennis' arm)
Tough break, my friend.

DENNIS

What do you mean?

COREY

Nothing. Let's go howl at the moon.

He exits, and Dennis follows.

Dean enters.

DEAN

Y'ever hear the term *tempest in a teapot?*

He lights a cigarette, his hands shaking slightly. He's in high emotional distress, but keeping it controlled.

DEAN

They use it to talk about uprisings. Make 'em sound weak. These little rebels, tempest in a teapot! I think all that power smashed and compressed in a teapot? I'd be pretty damn scared of that teapot. A tempest is a storm, bad one, wind and rain to sink a ship. But there's a play about a tempest, and when they talk about the storm, they talk a lot about fire.
(abrupt surge in energy)
The fire and cracks of sulfurous roaring! All afire with me! I flamed in amazement!
(back to himself)

DEAN (cont'd)

That's the little spirit that starts the whole mess. He's on fire, and he leaves everything behind him on fire. That sounds pretty powerful, even in a teapot.

Nick enters, unkempt. We're in his bungalow.

NICK

It's nice to see you, James. I was wondering when you'd be by.

DEAN

There's an operation in Nevada, Operation Teapot, dropping nukes. Trying to make 'em stronger. Last one only killed two hundred thousand Japanese, next one's gotta be even worse. What d'ya think it'd be like? Gettin' bombed.

NICK

I try not to think about it.

DEAN

What would you do? If you knew your time was about to run out, if you could see death coming over the hills. Would you sit and wait? Try to – outrun it, maybe?

NICK

I really try never to think about it.

DEAN

Never think about Japan? You must'a been, what, 35? Where were you when Japan went...
(makes explosion sound)

NICK

I was working on a musical, getting it ready/for Broadway.

DEAN

You were home already?

NICK

I was disqualified from military service. Bad heart.

DEAN

What's the matter with your heart?

NICK

Oh, ah, what did they call it?/Something like –

DEAN

You don't know what's wrong with your own heart?

NICK
(eager to change the subject)
It was a long time ago. I got what you asked for. A closed set, and we're shooting in color.

DEAN

I know. So I'm gonna do the picture.

NICK
(relieved grin)
Thank goodness.

DEAN

I came to say goodbye. This is the last time you'll see me 'til we wrap.

NICK

You're doing the method?

DEAN

Next time you see me, I'll be him.

NICK

Is that why you've been so…

DEAN

You ever see photos of a guy after he ran a marathon?

NICK

They look like they're about to shrivel up and blow away.

Dean nods.

NICK

You can trust me. I hope you know that.

Dean considers him.

NICK

You can hold the wheel. Do what it takes to feel safe. I'll be there to help.

DEAN

I oughta be gettin' on. Seems like someone's back in bed might like you gettin' on, too.

NICK

Be seeing you, James. Thank you. We'll make a masterpiece.

DEAN

You're goddamn right. We better.

> *Nick looks him over, but Dean is lost in thought. Nick exits. Dean starts shifting his body, his posture.*

> *Figment C enters and takes Dean's glasses off his face, speaking to Dean like the devil on his shoulder as Dean experiments, finding his new self.*

FIGMENT C

An undercover army has betrayed American respect for law and order.

> *Figment E enters and takes Dean's turtleneck off, revealing a white T-shirt.*

FIGMENT E

It is the solemn duty of every citizen to work for the building of youth fortified against temptation.

> *Figment A and Figment D enter,*
> *holding a red windbreaker. They help*
> *Dean put it on.*

FIGMENT D

Boys from eight to eleven years old are already turning toward delinquency.

FIGMENT A

Already filled with hatred and spite against their society.

> *Dean completes his transformation into*
> *Jim, the role he'll inhabit the rest of*
> *this act.*

FIGMENT B

A mother cried, *What did I do wrong?*

FIGMENT C

A father did everything he knew how, yet he failed

> *Dean puts his head up and falls back*
> *into the arms of the figments. They*
> *hoist Dean up to carry him above,*
> *speaking to him, inspiring him,*
> *embodying the spirit of speed as they*
> *carry him along. He's weightless, lost in*
> *the rush, euphoric and intoxicated,*
> *refueling.*

FIGMENT A

Boys as young as ten are already filled with hatred!

FIGMENT B

Filled with spite against their society!

FIGMENT C

The mysteries of life no longer remain a mystery to the juvenile!

FIGMENT E

He considers himself grown up, smart, above the law!

The figments move Dean about, his
body flying weightless and free.

FIGMENT D

We must adopt the methods of warfare and fight for the youth of
our country.

FIGMENT C

Against this faceless traitor, juvenile delinquency, that seeks to
destroy our institutions.

FIGMENT A

It cuts from within.

FIGMENT B

It has only selfish purposes.

FIGMENT C

This is the antagonist of everything honorable in our present day.

FIGMENT A

The public is enraged. They want action.

FIGMENT D

Something is rotten at the core of our culture.

FIGMENT E

The fight against juvenile delinquency is necessary for the
preservation of the American way of life.

FIGMENT C

Not even the communist conspiracy could devise a more effective
way to demoralize our citizens.

FIGMENT B

This is not a passing phenomenon

FIGMENT E

This a dark, and all too real facet of what our society has become.

> *The figments surge, carrying Dean over*
> *hills and around bends as they carry*
> *him offstage.*
>
> *Dennis enters, smoking a cigarette,*
> *pacing, angry.*

DENNIS

Hours. *Hours* he was in his trailer the first night. He went in with two bottles of wine, then –

> Ride of the Valkyries *blasts from*
> *offstage.*

DENNIS

And then the music! Louder than a goddamn construction site! Over and over! Meanwhile, we're just out there waiting for him to do the job he was gettin' paid for!

> *Natalie enters.*

DENNIS

I don't mind waiting when a director asks me to, but when it's some diva keeping me out all night…

NATALIE

He and Nick, they're *artists*. We have to respect the process.

DENNIS

Process? He skips rehearsal to go get drunk – if that's genius, Shakespeare's rolling in his grave.

NATALIE

It'll be worth it.

DENNIS
(brandishing script)
And there isn't even anything in the goddamn script! What does he need to prepare for?
(reading)
Jim enters and lies down on the street, he goes to sleep as the opening credits play.
We coulda been foolin' around at my place two hours ago!

NATALIE

Fooling around?

DENNIS

Well, I was hoping you/wanted –

NATALIE

I've actually been thinking we/should –

DENNIS

Don't you – we have fun, don't we?

> *She laughs, grabs his hand, and kisses his knuckles. Dean enters, staggering slightly.*

DEAN

Nick! Nickyyyy!

> *Nick enters.*

NICK

Are we ready?

> *Dean nods, more than a bit tipsy.*
> *Corey enters and stands with Dennis and Natalie.*

                              COREY
Are they shooting?

                             DENNIS
Yeah, let's see what all the goddamn fuss is about.

                              NICK
All right, let's clear everybody.

                Corey, Natalie, and Dennis back off.

                              DEAN
Just lemme do something, 'kay? I'll play around a little. You just roll.

                              NICK
Of course, Jim.

                *Natalie, Corey, and Nick fade back
                offstage. Dennis goes to the edge of the
                wings but remains onstage.*

                *Dean walks downstage, places a doll
                on the ground, then walks upstage.*

                          NICK *(offstage)*
And...ACTION!

                       Dean winces.

                              DEAN
No! No, no, just...don't shout, just gimme a little silent little – just –
                       (finger to his lips)
Shh. Just gimme a go-ahead.

                          NICK *(offstage)*
Of course. I'm sorry, Jim.

                Dean nods. Dennis rolls his eyes.

Dean takes a moment, then staggers downstage. He collapses forward onto his stomach. He rolls onto his side and smiles at the doll. He picks it up and whispers, hello, *then gives it a kiss and nestles it in the crook of his arm. He cuddles it, pulls his knees to his chest, whispers a lullaby, and then lies still, starting to doze.*

All the while, Dennis watches Dean work. At the start, he has a chip on his shoulder. As he watches, the chip disappears. He realizes something special is happening. His eyes go wide and he watches, rapt.

After a moment Dean sighs and then sits up.

> DEAN

OK. All done.

> NICK *(offstage)*

Cut!

Nick, Natalie, and Corey reenter. Nick claps. Dennis starts to clap, too, but he notices Natalie and Corey aren't and he controls himself.

> NICK

Beautiful, Jim. Really beautiful.

He goes to Dean, unsure how to help as Dean pushes himself up. He tries to put his arm around Dean's shoulders, but Dean shrugs him off and exits.

Dennis looks at Corey and Natalie.

> DENNIS

What the hell was that?

> COREY

That's called improvisation, my good man.

> DENNIS

Where the hell did it *come* from?

> NATALIE

It came from *him*. That's what I've been trying to tell you.

Dennis nods, considering.

> NICK

All right, that's a wrap for tonight, friends. I'll see you tomorrow morning. Get some rest.

He and Corey exit. Natalie glances after Nick.

> NATALIE

Listen, I might be a little busy/for a while.

> DENNIS

Yeah, sure.

He's lost in thought, looking where Dean disappeared.

> NATALIE

Maybe we could meet at Googie's for a malted later on? Talk about/the day?

Dean wanders on with a rucksack.

> DENNIS
> (watching Dean, distracted)

Uh-huh. Sounds swell.

NATALIE

OK. See you in a while.

She waits for him to speak, then exits.

DENNIS

Hey!

He rushes to Dean and grabs his elbow.

DENNIS

Listen, I gotta talk to you!

Dean pulls his arm away.

DEAN

Talk to someone else. I got places to be.

He starts to leave.

DENNIS

Please! You gotta teach me how to do that!

Dean waits, then turns.

DENNIS

That was the greatest minute of acting I've seen in my entire life. I seen guys do *To be or not to be* without half the art you just put into lying on the damn *street!* You gotta teach me how to do that!

DEAN

You don't wanna know how to do that.

He starts to leave again.

DENNIS

I do! I need to be a great actor!

Dean turns back.

DEAN

Need to? Why?

DENNIS

Because there's this hurt in me and I gotta let it out!

> *Dean is struck. Dennis starts talking*
> *quickly off the cuff, trying to keep*
> *Dean's attention.*

DENNIS

All my life, I was a nobody from nowhere. The only thing that ever made it better was to *make* something, make people say, *wow!* My parents are miserable, they take it out on me, so I was miserable. But – when I put something *into* the world – it's the only way I ever felt like I was *filling* space, not – taking it up.

> *He realizes he's rambling. Dean nods.*

DENNIS

I'm gonna try and do like you either way. But I won't know what I'm doing.

DEAN

Sounds dangerous.

> *He considers, then walks downstage.*

DEAN

You comin'?

> *Dennis hustles over. Dean sits on the*
> *edge of the stage. Dennis sits next to*
> *him. Dean lights a cigarette.*

DENNIS

You were in The Actors Studio in New York, right?

DEAN

Youngest cat they ever took.

DENNIS

So that's where you learned?

DEAN

Learned what? The method?

DENNIS

That what they call it?

DEAN

(nods)
They try to teach it. But that's not where I learned it.

Dean offers him a cigarette, Dennis accepts.

DEAN

It's not something you get taught. You do it to yourself. Crack your ribs, tear away everything, find the roots of you. Then you collect the lives around you, absorb everyone. So when you act, you're not *pretending*, you're *producing*. You keep shaving down, shaping, you never finish creating yourself.

DENNIS

Wow. That's – a whole lot.

DEAN

Sure is. So it's like learning to walk, it just happens once your mind's ready. You can't be worryin' about the script, remembering what you have to repeat like a goddamn parrot. Every line, it's gotta be the first time you ever said it and the last time you ever will.

DENNIS

But you do it again and again, different angles, and –

DEAN

Yup.

                    DENNIS
And every time is the first time?

                    DEAN
Yup.

                    DENNIS
That sounds exhausting.

                    DEAN
            (deep breath)
Yup.

            Dennis considers.

                    DENNIS
Then that's what I'll do.

            Dean looks at him, then laughs.

                    DEAN
Christ, I just handed you a loaded gun.
            (sigh)
All right. I'll teach you how to use it. Shit.

                    DENNIS
Really? Wow, OK. Great.

            Dean stands up.

                    DENNIS
So why'd *you* need to? Be an actor, I mean.

            Dean considers a moment.

                    DEAN
When I was nine, my mom died. My dad abandoned me, so I rode a
train across the country to Indiana to live with an aunt and uncle I

DEAN (cont'd)

never knew. Rode the whole way next to her casket, touching it and missing her and not knowing how I'd live. Without that part of me.

He moves around, using the space.
Dennis watches.

DEAN

And at night, I'd sneak out, and I'd run through the fields and the forest 'til I was at the cemetery. I'd climb over the wall and stand six feet on top of her, nine years old. And I'd cry and I'd *scream. Goddamnit Mom, why'd you LEAVE me? I NEEDED you! What was WRONG with me? I'm special, Mom! And you're gonna look down and I'm gonna be so goddamn great and I'm gonna do it ALL ON MY OWN!*

He's heaving from the emotional
exertion, then calms down, takes out
another cigarette.

DENNIS
(hushed)

Wow.

DEAN

So you got anything to shoot tomorrow?

DENNIS

A couple lines in the fight scene.

DEAN

Good. We'll do some work then.

He turns to go.

DENNIS

Hey, I'm gonna go meet Natalie at Googie's. You know it?

DEAN

It's not gonna be that kinda thing, pal. I'll see ya tomorrow.

Natalie enters and sits at the booth at
Googie's. Dean exits. Dennis watches
him go, buzzing with excitement, then
walks to Natalie.

DENNIS

Hey, sorry I kept you waiting. I was just off with Dean, talking about
the craft and all.

NATALIE

That's OK, I was with Nick. I've been helping him a lot, finding the
voice for the picture.

DENNIS

Sure. You wanna go somewhere? Get a bottle/and fool around?

NATALIE

Dennis, you know we're just friends, right?

DENNIS

Yeah, of course. Did you think I thought we were –
                    (ironic)
goin' steady?

NATALIE

No – it's not about that. I like you so much. I just don't want you to
think I'm someone/I'm not.

DENNIS

Hey, I'm busy, I'm gonna be working with Dean, you're – doin' what
you're doin' with Nick.

NATALIE

It's not so scandalous!

DENNIS

Hang on, are you messing around with Nick? That's illegal!
He's/gotta be -

NATALIE

And is it legal when you and I/fool around?

DENNIS

That's pretty goddamn different!

NATALIE

I suppose you think I'm disgusting?

DENNIS

Hey, look, you're on your journey, I'm on mine.

NATALIE

Just say what you think of me!

DENNIS

I think you're a good kid/I just think you –

NATALIE

Stop saying *kid!* For the love of *God!*

DENNIS

So you want me to leave?

NATALIE

Do you want to stay?

DENNIS

Well, c'mon, I'll drive you home.

NATALIE

I'm a big girl, I can take care of myself!

DENNIS

(plaintive)

What about how I make you feel safe?

> *Natalie turns from him. He exits. She
> slumps.*

*Figment E and C enter and sit down
at Natalie's table, conducting an
interview as she sulks.*

FIGMENT E
(a tweedy interviewer)
Doctor, you are undoubtedly in a position to give our readers some insight. Is there any way of measuring the cost of juvenile delinquency?

FIGMENT C
(a conservative, stern doctor)
How does one measure the cost of wasted years?

Natalie covers her ears.

FIGMENT E
What would you say are the factors most responsible for juvenile delinquency?

FIGMENT C
Some youngsters are eager for adventure. Others follow the code of the street because mischief is infectious. These are the easy cases.

*The two figments start crowding
Natalie as they talk, taking up more of
the table.*

FIGMENT E
What about the hard cases?

FIGMENT C
There are boys and girls who have grown up without ever feeling wanted or loved.

*Their voices begin to grow unnaturally
loud. Natalie curls up into her corner
of the booth, clamping her hands over
her ears.*

FIGMENT E

I often wonder whether the common problems all youngsters face might contribute to delinquency.

FIGMENT C

Adolescence is a shock. This is a time when boys and girls are trying terribly hard to discover who they are. The insecurity and inadequacy which comes with this makes some lash out aggressively.

> *Figment E becomes more and more at home, leaning on Natalie, crushing her.*

FIGMENT E

Why has juvenile delinquency become such a major social problem today, Doctor?

FIGMENT C

Youths today started life with fathers at war. Families are on the move, millions of them pulling up roots. Homes are smaller, cities more crowded. There aren't attics or back yards to play in. For years there has been tension about what's ahead for all of us. War or peace? Depression or prosperity?

> *Natalie bursts up and rushes offstage. Figment C and E snap back into their professional bearing.*

FIGMENT E

What can be done to combat this trend of delinquent youth?

FIGMENT C
(chuckle)
We are quite a long way from having that kind of wisdom.

> *Figments C and E exit.*

> *Corey and Dean enter from opposite wings. They're both in character. Corey is cocky, Dean is guarded.*

COREY *(in character)*
Best we set some ground rules, eh?

> *Natalie and Dennis enter in character
> and stand behind Corey, who takes out
> a switchblade.*

COREY *(in character)*
We're not here to do lethal damages –
(jabs hard with knife)
Isn't that right?

DENNIS *(in character)*
Yeah, just a little scratch!

COREY *(in character)*
We're just havin' fun!

> *Dennis laughs cruelly.*

DEAN
Hey, let's cut, huh?

> *Nick enters.*

NICK
Yup, cut! That's a cut!

> *Corey puts up his hands—What the
> hell? Dean gestures at Dennis, who
> goes to him.*

DEAN
(quiet)
I saw you planning to laugh.

DENNIS
Oh. No, I just figured/since I –

DEAN

Exactly, you *figured.*

NICK

Everything all right over there?

DENNIS

We're fine!

DEAN

Give us a second, huh?
(to Dennis)
Don't plan a reaction. Strip away. Simple reality.

DENNIS

You're right. Got it. Thanks.

> *Dean feels brushed off. Dennis steps
> away.*

NICK

Are we ready to try again?

> *Dean looks around, hustles offstage,
> returns with a tire iron. He saunters to
> Natalie.*

DEAN

Boy, would ya take a look at that?

> *He holds it out. She takes it.*

COREY

What's going on, Nick?

> *Nick holds a hand up to Corey—*
> Patience.

DEAN

It's great, huh?

                              NATALIE
What?

                               DEAN
Wrapping your hand around something so big and *hard*?

>   *Natalie is mortified and drops the tire*
>   *iron. Dennis laughs, shocked. Dean*
>   *points at him.*

                               DEAN
There! You can't fool a camera, my friend.

                               NICK
We're losing daylight, Jim.

                               DEAN
All right, let's go.

>   *He picks up the tire iron.*

                               DEAN
I'm usin' this.

>   *They get reset and Nick exits.*

                         NICK *(offstage)*
Action!

                      COREY *(in character)*
Best we set some ground rules, eh?

>   *Dean takes a swipe at him with the*
>   *tire iron.*

                      COREY *(in character)*
We're not here to do lethal damages –
                    (jabs hard with knife)
Isn't that right?

                    DENNIS *(in character)*
Yeah, just a little scratch!

                    COREY *(in character)*
We're just havin' fun!

                    Dennis laughs more naturally. Corey
                    steps towards Dean, who slips away.

                    COREY *(in character)*
Hey, I thought we were gonna play! What'sa matter? You soft?

                    Dean shrieks in rage, tosses the tire
                    iron. He takes out a switchblade and
                    swipes at Corey.

                    COREY *(in character)*
Aha! That's more like it!

                    They swipe at each other, jump away.
                    Corey taunts Dean, the duel getting
                    serious, until Corey lands a jab that
                    slices Dean behind the ear. Dean
                    grunts in pain, touches his head. He's
                    bleeding. A fire enters his eyes, he
                    prepares to take a swipe, but Nick
                    rushes on.

                         NICK
Cut! Cut! We need a medic!

                         DEAN
                    (furious)
God DAMN it!

                         NICK
Don't worry, Jim. We'll/get it –

                        DEAN
Don't EVER call cut when I'm in a real moment! Why the HELL did
you bring me/here?

                        NICK
How about we take five?

                        DEAN
Do you know what you just DID to me? Don't you EVER do that
again!

                        COREY
Who's the director here?

                        DENNIS
He's got a process.

                        COREY
And a screw loose.

            He exits.

                        NICK
We are taking five, Dennis!

            Dennis looks to Natalie. She ignores
            him and exits.

                        DENNIS
            (to audience)
So we took five. And they had it out.

            He exits. Dean is shaking with anger
            and distress, and as Nick approaches,
            he shirks away.

                        DEAN
I got it under control!

NICK

We can't make a picture this way. You do see that, right?

Dean paces, not meeting his eyes.

NICK

You'll make both of us look like fools.

DEAN

(sharp laugh)

Both of us?

NICK

The others take their cues from you. And they need faith in their director. So what will it take?

DEAN

Let me do my work! You're jangly and weird like a scared kid! It gets inside me!

NICK

If I stay out of your way, you'll help me keep a professional set?

DEAN

(tormented)

I can't be doing this to myself for no reason!

NICK

I'll stay calm and reserved, and you'll be a stabilizing influence? Can we call that a deal?

He holds out his hand. Dean considers.

NICK

Tension is natural. It's necessary for good work. But we can't have anything festering.

Dean shakes Nick's hand.

NICK

Clear your head for a minute and we'll start fresh.

Dean nods, exits. Nick exits opposite.
Dennis enters, walks to center stage,
looks at the audience.

DENNIS

It lasted a good —
(does some mental math)
Three or four days. Then…

He exits. Corey, Dean, and Natalie
enter.

COREY *(in character)*

All right, softie, you know the rules of chicken? When Judy gives the signal, we go full steam ahead, and whoever swerves first is the loser.

DENNIS *(in character)*

Or else — SMASH!

COREY *(in character)*

That's right, disaster. Do we understand the stakes?

DEAN *(in character)*
(dismissive)

Get on with it, I have places to be.

COREY *(in character)*

A little luck, Judy?

Natalie smiles and kisses his cheek.

DEAN *(in character)*

Well hey, I could use some luck, too.

NATALIE'S MOTHER *(offstage)*

CUT!

*Natalie's mother storms on. Natalie is
mortified.*

NATALIE'S MOTHER

We will cut on this scene, thank you!

*She grabs Natalie's arm. Nick runs
on, barely keeping his panic controlled.*

NICK

Yeah, cut! Cut, everyone take five, thank you!

*Corey sighs and exits. Dennis hesitates,
then exits.*

DEAN
(startled, upset)

What is this?

NICK

Everything's fine, Jim.

NATALIE'S MOTHER

Nothing is fine! The things I hear do NOT constitute an acceptable
public image for a young GIRL!

NATALIE

I'm *not* a girl, Mother!

NATALIE'S MOTHER

Then why do I hear these things about you being treated like a
TART?

DEAN

Listen/Missus –

NATALIE'S MOTHER

Is it you? I know they say you are a maniac. And I know someone on
THIS set/is –

Nick rushes to the wings.

NICK

Dennis! Dennis, get over here a minute, huh?

Dennis enters.

DENNIS

Hey, what's/the –

NICK

This is a workplace!

DENNIS

I know.

NICK

And THUS, inappropriate fraternization with costars is FORBIDDEN. Is that CLEAR?

> *Everyone is listening closely. Dennis is confused.*

DENNIS

What about the whole, *this is a family, go/out and* –

NICK

Everyone knows about you and Natalie, and I am putting a stop to it RIGHT now!

DENNIS
(glancing at Dean)
There's nothing to stop, we're friends. We're hardly friends!

NICK
(harsh laugh)
I don't know how things work in *Kansas*, but in Hollywood, your reputation is your bond, and word travels *fast*. So if you expect to have any sort of future, you'd best quit it with – deviant distractions!

DENNIS

I'm here to do the work, I'm not distracted with/anything.

NICK

How about I call Warners up and see what they think about you carrying on with a high school girl?

Dennis looks around, getting the idea.

DENNIS

(sneering)

Whatever you say, *sir.*

NICK

You get your ass out of my sight!

He rushes to Natalie's mother and confers. Dennis is embarrassed, but walks away. Dean grabs his elbow.

DEAN

You know the La Brea Tar Pits? On Wilshire by the museum? Meet me there after we wrap.

Dennis nods and stalks off.

NATALIE

Are you happy now, Mother?

NATALIE'S MOTHER

I will wait for you in the car.

NATALIE

I don't need/you to —

NATALIE'S MOTHER

I will see you in the car.

She exits. Nick rushes over to Dean.

                              NICK

Jim, could we/talk about –

                              DEAN

No.

> *He turns away. Nick looks around,*
> *exposed, and exits. Natalie sits on a*
> *box, puts her face in her hands. Dean*
> *sits next to her.*

                            NATALIE

I can't do this.

> *Dean doesn't speak, but he's listening.*

                            NATALIE

I'm the little girl in pigtails.

                              DEAN

So you're green. Don't you know how good green looks on camera?

> *Natalie looks up at him, then smiles.*

                            NATALIE

Thank you, James.

> *Dean stands, puts a cigarette in his*
> *mouth.*

                              DEAN

It's Jim.

> *They exit. Figments A and D enter.*

                          FIGMENT A

Being of the youth of today, it is my sincere belief that juvenile delinquency is overrated.

FIGMENT D

Teenagers who are a betterment to the community outnumber the delinquents about 100 to 1.

FIGMENT A

There are *some* ill deeds committed by teenagers, but these cases have been given entirely too much publicity, which hurts the reputation of our whole country.

FIGMENT D

Young American citizens of today have many more opportunities than ever before.

FIGMENT A

Don't let a few ruin the great leaders of tomorrow.

Dennis enters and paces the stage,
angry but powerless.

FIGMENT D

A great deal of emphasis is placed on a very small minority of our youth.

FIGMENT A

All one reads about in magazines and papers is *What Are We Going to Do About Our Teenagers?*

FIGMENT D

It should be *What Are We Going to Do About Our Adults?*

Dean enters, goes upstage, stares into
the distance.

FIGMENT A

If we want to curb juvenile delinquency, we should start with their parents.

FIGMENT D

So the solution is for adults to put trust and faith in us, and America will have a greater tomorrow.

*They exit. Dennis' pacing brings him
to Dean.*

DEAN

The pits are natural tar, it seeps up from the ground. For thousands'a years, WAY before people, animals'd wander in, get stuck. And the tar would harden, and the wind and rain would tear at them 'til they were stripped to the bones. The bones melt down and they become tar, too. Poor bastards were just doing what came natural.

DENNIS

That's wild.

DEAN

You get knocked down enough, your guts strip away. You can't act without guts.

DENNIS

You mean today with Nick?

DEAN

You need *respect* if you want to be great. And nobody just gives it to you. You gotta *demand* it.

DENNIS

You think Nick doesn't respect me? Does a director even/*have* to –

DEAN

He's tryin' to be a kid again. He's a drunk, he's blown two marriages, our set's his playground. If this picture's good, it won't be on account'a of him.

DENNIS

What do you think I should do?

DEAN

You should quit worrying what *other* people think you should do.

DENNIS

So – should I fight him or something?

Dean sighs and lights a cigarette.

DEAN

We're all doomed. If those animals had fought, best they woulda done is break an ankle. You believe in fate?

DENNIS

I don't know.

DEAN

I believe in destiny, but I think we create it. And soon as we're born, our end's just waitin' for us to catch up.

DENNIS

So what should I do?

DEAN

You gotta escape with your guts. And I got places to be.

He leaves before Dennis notices.

DENNIS

Sure. Thanks.

*He realizes Dean is gone, and stares
off, thinking. Nick enters.*

NICK

All right, cats, we are moving on.

Natalie and Corey enter.

NICK

Crane shot next, so go have a smoke while we set up. Don't go far, we only have time for a few takes, when the crane's gone, it's gone. And we need this shot!

He laughs and exits. Dean enters and
watches from a distance.

DENNIS
I'm gonna go grab a hot dog. Anyone else?

NATALIE
Nick said to stay close.

DENNIS
Yeah, Nick's just full of bright ideas, huh?

COREY
Can't we have one day without/dramatics?

DENNIS
I'm hungry! There's a cart right outside, I'll be back in two shakes.

NATALIE
Dennis, *please* don't.

Dennis exits. A reporter enters,
approaching Dean.

REPORTER
James! I'm with Variety, thank you SO much for inviting me. I know you have a closed set.

DEAN
It seemed right to share a glimpse of our very special production.

REPORTER
So what's the scene you're filming today?

DEAN
One of the last, a real tempest in a teapot kinda scene.

REPORTER
And your character, is he coming to life very much as he was first envisioned?

DEAN

When characters are *envisioned*, they're too false. You have to strip down, find the simple reality.

Nick enters.

NICK

All right, we are ready! Let's get in place, everyone!

*Natalie looks for Dennis. Corey rubs
his face, angry.*

REPORTER

So you continue developing the character as you film?

DEAN

It always continues.

NICK

Wait a minute, where's Dennis?

Natalie looks away, distraught.

COREY

He said he'd be right back.

*Nick is shocked. He sees the reporter,
tries to be calm.*

REPORTER

Is something wrong over there?

DEAN

Oh, Nick has some –
             (waves hand dismissively)
You got any more questions?

REPORTER

Well, how much can you really develop as you shoot? Once it's on film, you can't change anything.

DEAN

Then it reminds you where you failed.

Nick starts pacing around, panicking.

NICK

Did he say *where* he was going? We need that little asshole or there's no shot!

The reporter watches Nick. Dean knows it.

DEAN

And you can start stripping away again.

NICK

God DAMN it. That's at least two takes gone already...

DEAN

Try to get back to that nice, simple reality.

NICK

We could still get one take. You only need one, right? Come on, he didn't just vaporize!

REPORTER

Is this sort of thing typical on one of Nick's sets?

DEAN

He's an unusual director, that's for sure.

Nick checks his watch.

NICK

And that's that.
(*getting angry*)

NICK (cont'd)

That's that.

*Dennis enters, wiping his face with a
napkin.*

DENNIS

Sorry I took a little bit, hope I didn't miss too much.

*Nick shakes with rage, trying to keep
under control.*

COREY

We couldn't get the shot, asshole. Really nice.

DENNIS

Oh, that's a pity! Did I cause much trouble?

NICK

I suspect you just cost Warners fifty thousand dollars.

DENNIS

Shucks!

*Nick, conscious of his surroundings,
walks to Dennis.*

NICK

You're fired. I never want to see your face again as long as I live.

*Dennis crumples his napkin, drops it
at Nick's feet.*

DENNIS

Funny thing – I'm under contract. And I hear Warners is happy with
that decision.

NICK

I can make one phone call to Warners/and tell them –

DENNIS

And I can make one and tell them about the way –
(voice getting steadily louder)
you conduct yourself with young actresses.

NICK

Dennis, I thought we were family.

Dennis shoves Nick's shoulder.

DENNIS

Well y'know how my family and I settle things?

He steps back, ready to fight. Nick
shakes his head.

NICK

You look like a buffoon. One day you're going to have to learn to use
your *brain*, Dennis.

He turns to leave.

DENNIS

Well what the hell's THAT mean?

NICK

That's a wrap for today everyone. Thank you for your time.
(turning back to Dennis)
Don't worry about remembering your lines. I have a feeling they'll be
on the cutting room floor.

He exits. Dennis looks to Dean for
approval. Dean holds his hand out for
the reporter, following her off.

COREY

My goodness, what a professional environment we're cultivating.

Corey exits. Natalie starts to go, too.

DENNIS

Wait!

She hesitates.

DENNIS

I had to do *something*. You get that, right?

NATALIE

Dennis, I can count on one hand the people in my life who aren't poisonous. I thought you were one. You made me feel safe. But the way you've made me feel lately? I think you might be the curse.

DENNIS

Hey, you don't have/to make –

NATALIE

I have to do whatever I feel like for a minute.

Dennis hesitates, then nods.

NATALIE

Did you know I was engaged last year?

DENNIS

No.

NATALIE

You never know how much you don't know. I *loved* that boy. Yes, we were just kids, but…and then my mother said I couldn't see him anymore. We didn't have a choice. So he put a bullet in his head.
(takes a moment)
He's alive, if you care. But he can't see me anymore. I used to think my curse meant I would die young, now I think I'm cursed to be covered in this slow poison. I need to rip it off where I can.

DENNIS

What if I apologize?

NATALIE

What if you change?

DENNIS

I can!

Natalie nods, thinking.

NATALIE

You're making that new Stevens Western next?

DENNIS

Yeah, Dean and me both. Shipping off for Texas soon as we wrap.

NATALIE

Here's my offer: you can call me one time. When you can prove you're not the curse. You make your case, I'll listen, but I'm the judge. If I you fail, we're done. So you better be sure.

DENNIS

I understand.

NATALIE

I'll see you at work tomorrow.

DENNIS

You need a ride?

NATALIE

(bitter)

My mother drives me.

She exits. Dennis turns to the audience.

DENNIS

You think this whole mess was my fault?

Dean enters, in character.

DENNIS/DEAN
(unison)
What was I supposed to do?

*Natalie enters in character. Dennis
exits as Natalie and Dean perform the
scene from her audition.*

NATALIE *(in character)*
It doesn't matter. People like that see what they want to see.

DEAN *(in character)*
Do you hate me, too?

NATALIE *(in character)*
I don't know what I feel anymore.

DEAN *(in character)*
(sigh)
Shame it all went sideways. This day started out so top-notch.

NATALIE *(in character)*
Why's that?

DEAN *(in character)*
I met you.

NATALIE *(in character)*
(anguished)
Just being around them makes me hate myself! I wish I could just live
for myself! Be who –

*Dean kisses her passionately, cutting
her off.*

NATALIE *(in character)*
Now what did you do that for?

DEAN *(in character)*
I couldn't help it.

NATALIE *(in character)*
I'm glad. So what do we do now?

DEAN *(in character)*
We can't go back to before.

NATALIE *(in character)*
I don't want to.

DEAN *(in character)*
Then I guess I better…keep on movin' forward.

He brings her close.

DEAN *(in character)*
Wanna come along?

NATALIE *(in character)*
More than anything in the world.

Nick, Cory, and Dennis enter.

NICK
(soft, emotional)
Cut.

*Dean and Natalie separate, her
emotional, him tired.*

NICK
My friends, that is a wrap. Congratulations. And thank you.

*Dennis and Corey shake hands. Dean
steps away, lights a cigarette. He's very
shaken.*

DENNIS
Hey, anyone wanna go celebrate? Malteds at Googie's?

*Nick whispers something to Natalie,
she grins.*

DENNIS

Nick? Whaddaya say?

Nick keeps whispering to Natalie.

DENNIS

Hey, I'm sorry about everything.

NICK

I know, Dennis. Believe me.

DENNIS

So? Malteds?

Natalie whispers to Nick.

NICK

Another time. Good luck in Texas.

*Nick and Natalie exit. Dennis turns
to Corey.*

DENNIS

Well hey, how about it?

COREY

Good night, Dennis. I hope you learn to use that brain before we end
up on another film together.

DENNIS

What the hell does that *mean?*

*Corey exits. Dennis turns to Dean,
who's wrung out. Dean takes out his
glasses and puts them on.*

DENNIS

I did like you said!

DEAN

What did I say?

DENNIS

To...get respect!

DEAN
(rhetorical question)
How'd it work out?

DENNIS

So teach me, then! You said/you would!

DEAN

I gotta go, pal. Picture's wrapped, I get to drive.

Even hollow and shaken, he grins.

DEAN

Gonna take a lotta driving this time. Better get started. Can't wait.

DENNIS

We can talk more in Texas. You taking the crew train?

DEAN

Buddy, I'm *drivin'*.

DENNIS

Maybe I could ride with you.

DEAN
(laugh)
If you saw how I drive, you wouldn't want any part of it.

DENNIS

Be careful.

DEAN

(grin)

Absolutely not.

> *He walks upstage, looking like he's
> run a marathon. He keeps his back to
> us, shivering.*

DENNIS

(to audience)

That was the first two months. I had three left.

> *Dennis exits. The figments enter and
> gather behind Dean. He falls back into
> their arms. They hoist him up. They
> become a car—or something like the
> spirit of speed—carrying Dean along.
> He's weightless, euphoric and relieved.
> His eyes are shut; his soul is refueling.*

> *The figments carry Dean off.*

END OF ACT.

ETHAN WARREN

ACT TWO

A TV host's voice booms from offstage.

TV HOST *(voice)*
Ladies and gentlemen, James Dean.

*Lights up on Dean in a chair, wearing
turtleneck and glasses. He smokes a
cigarette. When he speaks, he mumbles.*

DEAN
Hi there.

TV HOST *(voice)*
James is off to Texas to film an exciting new epic Western, but
before he goes, we asked him here to talk a bit about something
important. Now, James, you're a racing man, is that right?

DEAN
Yeah, I'm a bit of a racer.

TV HOST *(voice)*
And how fast can you go on the race track?

DEAN
Oh, I been clocked about a hundred'n eight, hundred'n nine.

TV HOST *(voice)*
And you've won a few races, haven't you?

DEAN
Once in a while, in between a picture. I showed all right in Palm
Springs last year.

TV HOST *(voice)*
Now James, we have a lot of young people watching at home. I was
hoping you'd say a little something about fast driving. Do you think
it's a good idea, driving fast on the highway?

Dean gets lost in thought. Then he sits forward.

DEAN

I used to like flyin' around. And that was dangerous. But I discovered racing, so now when I drive on the highway, I'm – real cautious. Cuz these cars are dangerous things. You can only drive 'em if you know just what you're doin'. You can't trust anyone but yourself.
(as he speaks, he becomes less and less convincing)
So I'm very cautious on the highway. I don't feel the need to drive fast. People think racing on a track is dangerous, but out there on the highway you're takin' your life in your hands.

He pauses, considering what he said.

DEAN

Well, I best be gettin' on down the road.

TV HOST *(voice)*

Do you have any parting words, James, for young people who want to drive like you?

Dean looks into the audience, a sly grin on his face.

DEAN

Hey, be careful out there, huh? I might be out on that road, and I sure like gettin' home safe!

The interviewer laughs heartily. Dean exits.

The figments file out and scatter themselves across the stage, beaming at the audience, delivering advertisements in their best '50s pitchman voices.

FIGMENT E

It's a new era in America, and this is a brand-new experience!

FIGMENT B

Drive in traffic with confidence, pass on the highway with safety. All these advantages, AND MORE, now available in all models!

FIGMENT D

Our new washer circulates and filters water to give you whiter, brighter clothes. It's a dream come true for any woman, because *progress* is our product!

FIGMENT C

Car racing is a brutal test, so only the BEST spark plugs can meet the challenge. When the chips are down, professional drivers turn to us. Don't you want that performance from *your* car?

FIGMENT A

Our revolutionary hair dressing won't grease-stain your hat! Hair experts said it couldn't be done!

FIGMENT B

Now you see what all the excitement's about!

FIGMENT C

Now you see the NEWEST new car of this generation, with new silhouette, new lines, new EVERYTHING!

FIGMENT E

Because *progress* is our product!

FIGMENT D

When the telephone was put in, everything seemed different. It wasn't just the calls I could make – people could call ME! I wasn't alone anymore!

FIGMENT A

Punch the light up to 80 feet farther down the road. You can't stop in time if you can't SEE in time!

FIGMENT D

Carpet fills any room with a special kind of warmth, comfort, and beauty. And it's so easy to buy on convenient budget terms!

FIGMENT C

Because *progress* is our product!

FIGMENT B

It's a man's dream to take the wheel of a powerhouse car and say, *I own it*. We fulfill this dream.

FIGMENT C

Did somebody say all ketchups taste the same? Why, the very IDEA!

ENSEBMLE E

Ours is the first and only tire with LIFE PROTECTOR safety! Your safety is our business!

FIGMENT A

Because *progress* is our product!

FIGMENT D

Today, top farmers are the ones who use machines in every phase of their operations.

FIGMENT C

Because progress is our product!

FIGMENT A

America's future DEPENDS on better and safer highways!

FIGMENT B

Because progress is our product!

FIGMENT C

What more could you want than that hearty flavor?

FIGMENT E

Because progress is our product!

FIGMENT D

But the greatest thrill of all comes just from driving it.

FIGMENTS E & B

Because progress is our product!

FIGMENTS E, B, & D

Progress is our product!

ALL FIGMENTS

PROGRESS IS OUR PRODUCT!

Beat.

FIGMENT E

And now, back to our program.

The figments clear, and Dennis enters.

DENNIS

(to audience)

We shot in this nothing little town in the middle of the Texan desert. That meant we got to take over, they rented out the one restaurant every night, they rented out the little cinema to watch the rushes after dinner, they rented out the whole entire hotel for us. Except the stars – that was Liz –

Liz enters

DENNIS

And Rock.

Rock enters and conspires with Liz, laughing.

DENNIS

Hollywood royalty, y'know, so they got private housing. Not that it was comfy, these rickety little shacks, but it was the best on offer. And lording over it all was – well, y'know about Stevens.

Stevens enters, wearing cowboy hat and
aviator sunglasses, examining papers.

DENNIS

Stern old Stevens. No-nonsense-on-my-set Stevens. That's how he
was supposed to be, at least. He had to be, on account of his bad
habit of going over budget and behind schedule. So he was – yeah,
stern no nonsense. At least that's how he was supposed to be.

Stevens reaches Liz and Rock, and he
cracks a joke to them. All three laugh.

DENNIS

Anyway. Dean got to town at the last minute. Of course.

Dean enters from the opposite wing,
nervous.

DENNIS

They had him sharing a house with Rock. I don't know whose idea of
a joke *that* was.

Rock sees Dean, sneers to himself, and
exits. Liz looks Dean over, and
follows Rock off.

DENNIS

And I guess first thing he did was find Stevens. I didn't see him until
a little later. Not until after some things had gone sour.

Dennis looks at Dean, then exits.
Dean goes towards Stevens.

DEAN

Mr. Stevens, hi. Good t'see ya.

Stevens looks up, placid.

DEAN

Do you have a few minutes to talk?

STEVENS

A very few.

DEAN

OK, well, I don't know if you talked to anyone, but I have sort of a process, things I need to/do –

STEVENS

I'm aware of your methods, yes.

DEAN

OK. Good. On my last picture, things got a/little bit –

STEVENS

It's my intention that this be a workplace, not a fraternity. I hope that's all right with you.

DEAN

That's how I want it. I want a real good, open, uh – forthright sorta/relationship –

STEVENS

James, I did not cast a matinee idol. I cast the shy unknown I met last year. In between, the world met you, and quite a lot changed. I understand. But I need that shy unknown to show up every day.

DEAN

Oh...well, I was hoping we could talk about how – what I need to do/could be –

STEVENS

I'm sure we'll find time. Right now, I have a very large crew to manage, and you should rest up.

> *Dean wants to push on, but Stevens*
> *levels a stern look at him, and Dean's*
> *mood turns.*

                         DEAN
That's how it'll be then, I guess.

                        STEVENS
Very good. I'll see you in the morning, James.

                    Dean sneers, and exits. Stevens'
                    shoulders slump. He takes off his
                    glasses, rubs his eyes. Stevens exits.
                    Rock enters with a cocktail shaker,
                    preparing for the evening. Dean reenters
                    and gives Rock a tense glance.

                         ROCK
James Dean, welcome to Texas. I don't think we've formally met,
have we?

                         DEAN
We did a TV project.

                         ROCK
Oh, that's right. You played, what, *Teenager 9?*

                         DEAN
What's your point?

                         ROCK
                    (feigning lightheartedness)
I'm pointless! I'm preparing a little happy hour, can I tempt you?

                    He holds up the cocktail shaker.

                         DEAN
That'll kill ya.

                         ROCK
If I'm going down, I'll go down happy. Would you like to take a load
off and talk about the picture? You'll be my nemesis, isn't that right?

                    Dean snorts, derisive.

DEAN

You sure did a lot of training, didn't you?

ROCK

What's YOUR point?

> *Dean chuckles. Rock is flustered.*
> *Dennis creeps onstage, hands in*
> *pockets, mimicking Dean.*

DEAN

Oh, Christ.

ROCK

What's the matter?

DEAN

This guy was on my last picture, he thinks he's my shadow now.

> *Dennis waits for Dean to welcome him.*

ROCK

Well you should invite him in, shouldn't you?

DEAN

Be my guest.

> *He exits. Rock goes to Dennis.*

ROCK

Hi there.

> *Dennis springs up, starstruck, unsure*
> *of who to be.*

DENNIS

Hi…I'm Dennis.

ROCK

Pleasure to meet you, Dennis. My name's Rock.

DENNIS

I know! Uh – yeah, I've seen your work.

ROCK

Well, I hope you enjoyed it. I'm afraid your friend James has hit the sack. Long trip, I guess.

DENNIS

Oh, ahright. Yeah, well, I guess/I'll just be –

ROCK

I was about to go visit our costar Liz for a round of drinks. Would you like to join us?

DENNIS

Really? She havin' a party?

ROCK

No, just a little intimate happy hour. We're old pals. We'd love to have you along.

DENNIS

Sure! Sounds great!

They start walking.

ROCK

So what role are you playing in our epic adventure?

DENNIS

I'll be your son, actually.

ROCK
(hearty laugh)
Well that certainly makes me feel old!

DENNIS

Sorry.

ROCK

Oh, it's an epic that spans generations, I suppose playing old is part of the deal. That's what makeup artists are for!

Stevens enters, still looking at papers.

ROCK

Have you met our illustrious director yet?

DENNIS

Not personally, no.

ROCK

Mr. Stevens!

Stevens looks up, smiling when he sees Rock.

ROCK

Can I introduce you to my son, Dennis?

STEVENS

Why, he's one of Warners' best and brightest new stars, isn't that right?

DENNIS

Oh! Uh – I don't know/about that.

STEVENS

I'm predicting a long, bright future, and we'll make sure this is a distinguished introduction.

He gives Dennis' hand a hearty shake and exits.

ROCK

He was in Germany, y'know, shooting the newsreel footage. He

ROCK (cont'd)

didn't even have to go, he volunteered. He doesn't make a big deal of it, never even mentions it. One of the greats.

DENNIS

Wow.

Liz enters as Dennis and Rock arrive.

ROCK

Bessie, darling!

LIZ

That you, Rockabye?

ROCK

But of course! And allow me to introduce Dennis, the fruit of our loins.

Dennis is star-struck.

LIZ

He's got your eyes.

ROCK

And your nose, lucky boy.

DENNIS
(small voice)
It's really nice to meet you.

LIZ

You as well! Did you bring the first round, Rocky?

ROCK

Do you really have to ask? Where are the glasses?

*Liz fetches glasses. Rock pours thick
brown cocktails.*

LIZ

Rock's specialty, a Chocolatini.

ROCK

Vodka, Hershey's syrup, and Kahlua.

LIZ

It's *divine*.

Rock hands them drinks. They toast.

ROCK

To the grandest old-fashioned epic to ever grace the screen, and Hollywood's three biggest stars!

LIZ

Cheers!

They clink, and drink.

DENNIS

Wow! That's something else!

ROCK

You know, Bess, Dennis worked on James Dean's last picture.

LIZ
(suddenly wary)

Is that right?

DENNIS

Yeah, it was – y'know, I had a good supporting part.

ROCK

So is it true what I hear about his…eccentricities?

DENNIS

He has sorta unusual techniques. It's how he does such good work.

ROCK

I've heard it's more like he takes up all the oxygen in the room.

DENNIS

Naw, he's just…y'know, unique. Talented.

Rock downs the rest of his drink.

ROCK

Drink up, my friend.

Dennis chugs. Rock refills his glass.

ROCK

I've seen a lot of actors try a lot of tricks, burn bright and flare out. Y'know who sticks around?

He hands Dennis a drink.

DENNIS

Who?

ROCK

The people who play for the team, don't steal scenes. Do right by their family.

DENNIS
(confused)

Oh.

LIZ

He means the studio, love.

Rock nods at Dennis, who drinks.

ROCK

When I showed up in Hollywood, just a scrawny punk from Illinois, you know who adopted me? Universal Pictures. They taught me how to speak, how to dress, they gave me a trainer and a nutritionist.

DENNIS

Wow.

ROCK

I learned to sing, dance, sword fight. That's more than my real family ever did. Isn't that right, Bess?

LIZ

I love my family, but MGM was home. My school, my social club, my world. And it still is.

She smiles and raises her glass.

DENNIS

So…solidarity with the team? That's how you succeed?

ROCK

That's the only way I've ever seen work, at least in the long term. Bess, do you have more hooch?

LIZ

Of course.

ROCK

Then you two need to pick up the pace!

Dennis drinks faster, turning to the audience.

DENNIS

Got a little hazy from there. He really wanted to know everything about Dean.

ROCK

So what did you mean about unusual techniques?

DENNIS

And…well, I guess I told him.

ROCK

(laugh)
That's pretty unusual! Pardon my French, but that is some *prickish* behavior.

DENNIS

I don't remember how I described it all. But I was mad! He blew me off!

ROCK

Honestly, I'm impressed you stood for that treatment at all, Dennis. You deserve better.

DENNIS

I was spinning, soon enough.

ROCK

Doesn't he deserve better, Bess?

LIZ

Everyone deserves to be treated with respect. Rocky my love, couldn't we talk about something else?

ROCK

It's important that Dennis know he's worth more than that!

DENNIS

Yeah!
(to audience)
I liked the sound of that!
(to Rock)
I like the sound of that!

He pushes himself up.

DENNIS

(to audience)
And then soon enough it was time to get home. We had an early morning.

*He staggers across to his room as Liz
and Rock exit.*

DENNIS

But first – I had a phone call to make.

*He sits down heavily, picks up the
phone.*

DENNIS

(sing-song)

Natalie! Natalie!

Beat.

NATALIE *(voice)*

What?

*Natalie enters, on the phone in LA,
her back to us.*

DENNIS

I'm cashing in my phone call! I been wanting to call but I waited 'til I
was sure everything's different!

NATALIE

What does that mean?

DENNIS

It means I know how I was wrong! I'm gonna be a real team player.

NATALIE

Are you drunk?

DENNIS

I was with my friends Rock and Liz, you mighta heard of them.
They're more like family t'me now.

NATALIE

Dennis, please say whatever you want to say very quickly.

DENNIS

I said it!

NATALIE

You didn't say anything.

DENNIS

I said I saw the error of my ways, and I know being a ball player and a good relationship with my colleagues is the best way to have a good life!

Natalie starts quietly crying.

DENNIS

Hey, what's happening there?

NATALIE

I was looking forward to hearing from you. I didn't think it would be perfect, but…better than this.

DENNIS

I'm doing my best!

NATALIE

I know. Please don't call me again.

DENNIS

Is it so bad what I did? I'm sorry!

NATALIE

It's not about you. Things in general are far less about you than you think.

DENNIS

What does THAT mean?

NATALIE

We had a deal, Dennis. Maybe I'll see you at a party sometime. Ignore me.

She hangs up.

DENNIS

HELLO?

Natalie's body shakes as she cries.

DENNIS

Bitch!

Natalie exits, crying. Dennis lies back, groaning. Figment A and Figment B enter, chatting.

FIGMENT A

Former Land Commissioner Bascom Giles took the witness stand on his own behalf in the trial charging him with stealing veterans land program funds.

FIGMENT B

West Texas wool growers will vote in the national referendum on the proposed wool advertising and promotional campaign cited in the National Wool Act of 1954.

Figments C, D, and E enter. They all move around, discussing in pairs and trios. Dennis stands and wanders among them. He tries to connect, but every time he moves too close, they slip away to evade him.

FIGMENT C

Ray Willoughby, widely known San Angelo rancher and banker, was reported recovering last night after undergoing major surgery.

FIGMENT D

Floodwaters receded rapidly Friday from the stricken border towns of El Paso and Juarez, leaving at least one person dead, several missing, and 11,000 flooded out of their homes.

FIGMENT E
Craig Hess, prominent Pecos farmer, died suddenly of a heart attack at his home around 4:30 PM Thursday. He was about 60 years old.

FIGMENT B
City Marshall Ben Royall asked city council to buy him a new billy club. His old one was worn out.

FIGMENT C
Jeremiah Thompson and his wife were killed, and their three children injured today when a truck struck their car 14 miles west of Amarillo.

*Pause to consider that. Then, moving
right along:*

FIGMENT A
A 50 percent reduction in the state's cotton acreage reserve was urged by the board of directors of the Texas Farm Bureau yesterday. The bureau wants the state reserve cut from 10 to 5 percent.

*The figments exit, leaving Dennis
defeated.*

DENNIS
(to audience)
Stevens made us all suit up and go to set, no matter if we had a scene. So I may have felt like a train hit me, but I had to be there bright and early to watch Dean and Liz shoot their first scene.

Liz enters, glamorous.

DENNIS
Somehow, she was fresh and shiny. Dean ran late, of course. That gave enough time for about a thousand curious Texans to assemble on the ridge to watch the big Hollywood production.

Liz smiles, and waves to the onlookers.

DENNIS

Not exactly a closed set. Dean wasn't thrilled, but he wasn't thrilled about much during that shoot.

Dean enters in cowboy hat and vest.
Dennis exits.

LIZ

Good morning, James. It's a pleasure to finally meet you.

Dean nods.

LIZ

I hope you don't feel you have to be nervous meeting/me.

When Dean speaks—and for the rest
of the shoot—he has a Texan drawl.

DEAN

I ain't.

LIZ

Oh. Good. I know I've done a lot of pictures, but we're about the same/age.

DEAN

I ain't nervous.

LIZ

Yes. Good.

DEAN

We gonna shoot this thing or not?

LIZ

Yes, Mr. Stevens said everything was just about right. He likes to/take his time.

*Dean goes to a box and sits. He slowly
draws knees to his chin, then brings his
feet down sharply, stamps on the
ground a dozen times, then jump into
the air and runs around screeching with
high-pitched, wild abandon. Liz
watches, disturbed. Finally, he stops.*

DEAN
(nodding off into distance)
Some audience up there, huh?

LIZ
Yes, well, everyone loves to get close to the magic of the movies.

DEAN
Never had an open set before.

LIZ
Is that right? Well, you needn't be nervous.

DEAN
My nerves are fine.

LIZ
Would you like to run the lines/a few times?

DEAN
'Scuse me.

*He walks upstage. With his back to
the audience, but exposed to the crowd,
he unzips his fly and urinates. Liz is
silently shocked. Dean turns back.*

LIZ
My, you must have been quite uncomfortable.

DEAN
Not in particular.

Liz is struck dumb. Dennis reenters.

DENNIS

They shot the scene.

DEAN *(in character)*

I'm not such a bad fella. I got enough people seem to like me.

LIZ *(in character)*

I'm sure I'll come to be one of them.

DENNIS

And they shot it again.

DEAN *(in character)*

I'm not such a bad fella. I got enough people seem to like me.

LIZ *(in character)*

I'm sure I'll come to be one of them.

DENNIS

And then they shot it again and again until I thought they'd collapse.

DEAN *(in character)*

I'm not such a bad fella. I got enough people seem to like me.

LIZ *(in character)*

I'm sure I'll come to be one of them.

DENNIS

Stevens must'a heard film stock was free.

Dean abruptly turns and exits.

DENNIS

And when we broke for lunch, he vanished.

Rock rushes on and goes to Liz.

ROCK

Are you all right?

LIZ

I'm fine.

ROCK

Dennis!

Dennis goes over.

ROCK

Is that kind of deviant behavior par for the course?

DENNIS

I never saw anything quite like that before.

ROCK

Well we need to go talk to Stevens! It's utterly unacceptable!

Dennis doesn't respond.

ROCK

Are you coming?

Dennis is anxious, reluctant to speak.

LIZ

I don't want to make trouble. Let's just go have a happy hour.

ROCK

Well I'm going to talk/to him.

LIZ

Rocky, *please.* I just want to go drink my damn lunch.

DENNIS
(to audience)
So that's what we did.

Rock steps offstage, returns with
cocktails.

DENNIS

Or they did. I couldn't keep up with those two sponges. And they
were *mad*.

ROCK

He's going to ruin this picture! I can't afford that! Dennis *certainly*
can't!

LIZ

There could be reporters here any time! I'll be in *Life* magazine next
to a bare-naked maniac!

DENNIS

And they wanted to do something about it.

ROCK

We won't be able to get him fired. The contracts are like straitjackets.

LIZ

Couldn't you get Stevens to bring his foot down?

ROCK

Yeah, down on the little pup's throat.

DENNIS

This was…not exactly what my ideal family would look like.

ROCK

Dennis! How would one go about making James Dean lose his
temper?

DENNIS

I was distracted, and tired, and sad. I guess I wanted someone to be
nice to me. So I said –
        (to Rock)
He hates feeling like he's wasting his effort. Feeling like he got all
geared up for nothing.

Rock and Liz pause, considering.

LIZ

(to Rock)
Well, I imagine you could work with that, couldn't you?

ROCK

I believe I could. Dennis –

But Dennis walks away.

DENNIS

(to audience)
I couldn't be part of that. I did a lot wrong. But not like that.
(shakes head, sighs)
So we went back to set.

*Dean and Stevens enter and work
begins again. Stevens addresses the
group, Dean lurks in the back.*

STEVENS

If we're all fed and fresh, we'll spend the afternoon on Liz's arrival.
Ready to meet the in-laws?

LIZ

But of course!

STEVENS

Then let's have a wonderful afternoon and give America the great big
film it deserves!

*He gives Dennis a hearty pat on the
back, starting to go. Liz and Rock go
upstage. Dean rushes to Stevens.*

DEAN

Listen, Mr. Stevens, if you won't be shootin' with me, it'd be
better/if I –

STEVENS

Please wait with the rest of the cast and crew. I may need you.

DEAN

You're gonna spend the rest of the day on this scene. If I just go/practice –

STEVENS

I have a policy, and it's not negotiable. Do not gum up the works.

> *He exits before Dean can respond.*
> *Dean paces in irritation. Rock goes*
> *and puts a hand on his shoulder.*

ROCK

Tough old salt, isn't he?

> *Dean shrugs away from Rock's grip.*

ROCK

Hot out today, too! But that's the life we chose, eh?

> *Dean grumbles.*

ROCK

I don't mind keeping the engine idle, of course. Do you, Dennis?

> *Dennis doesn't respond. Rock looks*
> *over at him.*

DENNIS

I'm fine.

> *Rock is frustrated by Dennis'*
> *noncommittal.*

ROCK

At least talent doesn't go stale if it sits out. Isn't that right?

*He puts a hand on Dean's shoulder,
and looks back to Dennis. Dennis
looks away.*

DEAN
(shrugging Rock off violently)
Gimme a little space! Ya mind?

ROCK
Of course! I know you have – what did you call them Dennis? Odd
methods?

Dean gives Dennis a sharp look.

DENNIS
I didn't!

ROCK
(hearty laugh)
Have a smashing afternoon, gents. Best be getting to work.

He goes upstage to Liz. Dean fumes.

DENNIS
I wasn't talking about you. I just said with Nick you used to –

DEAN
It's not about you.

DENNIS
Yeah. I know.

He walks away. Stevens reenters.

STEVENS
OK, everyone to first positions. This scene is the rest of our day,
we'll be getting it right.

DEAN
So you're not gonna need me!

STEVENS
James, I absolutely do not have time for this.

DEAN
I don't have time! How are you so DENSE? I gotta be/careful!

STEVENS
James! You are dangerously close to being held in contempt of your
workplace!

DEAN
Then I'm in contempt! I have contempt for you and this picture and
ALL of this!

STEVENS
(getting closer)
I'm happy to have you removed to the medical tent if you're
hysterical. Otherwise *sit down.*

Dean fumes, then snaps a Sieg Heil.

DEAN
Yes, mein Führer!

Stevens' face falls.

STEVENS
Do you know the significance of that gesture?

DEAN
It means you're a goddamn dictator!

STEVENS
You are incorrect. Do me the courtesy of never again speaking to me
unless you are spoken to.

*He exits quickly. Liz and Rock
hesitate, then exit, too. Dennis has
been watching from the corner. Dean
looks around, then goes to Dennis.*

DEAN

You get a load'a that?

DENNIS

*(shocked and excited to have Dean's
attention)*

Yeah, uh, that was wild.

DEAN

Like we're his goddamn robots! He has no idea how hard it is, what
we do!

DENNIS

He's under a lot of pressure.

DEAN

Is that what he told you? Yeah, they butter you up, run you down,
and then you do bad work!

DENNIS

So what're you gonna do?

DEAN

That's the question.

He shakes his head, at a loss.

DENNIS

You worried you're gettin' stuck in the tar?

DEAN

It's all our careers on the line, not just mine. But he won't talk to me!

DENNIS

I could try. We have a good thing going.

DEAN

You can't talk to a man like that. You gotta *show* him.

DENNIS

I don't wanna lose my lines again…

DEAN

Your part's just as important as mine, you're not gettin' cut outta this one.

DENNIS

You think I'm a co-lead?

DEAN

Hell yeah! And this is your make or break moment.

DENNIS

You think I could get away with something like I pulled with Nick?

DEAN

You got away with that, didn't you?

DENNIS

I want a good reputation, though.

DEAN

Who gives a shit about a reputation? I gotta go clear my head. You wanna come along?

DENNIS

Yeah? Sure!

STEVENS *(offstage)*

Please keep the noise down in the peanut gallery! We are trying to work!

DEAN

See? And this is day one!

DENNIS

You got something in mind?

DEAN

Let's go clear our heads.

He and Dennis exit together.

Liz enters, talking on the phone.

LIZ

Darling, it's *not* a lie! There simply isn't space! The motel is booked, and -...yes, I have a house but there isn't space for both you and - ...Do you really not trust me? When have I ever given you - ...You never let me finish a sentence...I'm sorry. Could I talk to the boys?...Please! I love you!
(trying not to cry)
Hello? HELLO? I hate this goddamn motion picture!

She gathers herself and exits.

The figments return, discussing national news in groups.

FIGMENT E

Senator Karl Mundt of South Dakota proposed that President Eisenhower add an improved farm program to his list of vital legislation.

FIGMENT B

Senate Democratic Leader Lyndon Johnson, who suffered a heart attack July second, was discharged Sunday from the Bethesda Naval Hospital.

FIGMENT D

Hurricane Connie headed on a course early Monday that should bring it into the United States mainland.

FIGMENT A

Governor Goodwin Knight of California listed Governor Averell

FIGMENT A (cont'd)

Harriman of New York as a strong contender to bid next year for the Democratic presidential nomination.

> *Dennis reenters, excited, and tries to*
> *connect with the figments, but as he*
> *approaches, they evade him.*

FIGMENT E

Visiting Russian leaders took a look at American farm machinery for nearly two hours on Monday.

FIGMENT D

Senators have demanded to know what the government intends to do to curb imports of foreign oil.

> *Dennis gives up, and just stands to the*
> *side, watching.*

FIGMENT B

The three-day search for Mrs. Wilma Allen came to a grisly end Sunday.

FIGMENT A

The 43-year-old mother of two was found in a dense hedge thicket 100 yards off US Highway 69.

FIGMENT E

Only a few miles from where Bobby Greenlease was killed less than two years ago.

FIGMENT D

Police Captain Jack Halvery said, *right now, we're in the blind as to the murderer.*

> *The figments take a moment to*
> *consider, then make their way offstage,*
> *ignoring Dennis, who's disappointed as*
> *he tries once more to connect with them.*

*Rock enters in character. Dennis gets
in character, too.*

ROCK *(in character)*
(drunken slurring)
You oughta take responsibility for your country, son! There's a war
on! Be a damn patriot!

DENNIS *(in character)*
There's other ways to help my country, Dad. And I'll be doing my
part the best way I know how.

ROCK *(in character)*
You ungrateful son of a – this isn't how I raised you!

DENNIS *(in character)*
You raised me to never be a follower, Dad, and I don't mean to start
following now. You better take it easy on that bourbon. It changes
you, and not for the better.

STEVENS *(offstage)*
Cut!

He enters.

STEVENS
All right, that was very good, very good. We're going to take it again.

DENNIS
If it was good, why are we takin' it again?

STEVENS
I need enough footage to be sure I've captured the best material!

*He claps Dennis on the shoulder and
laughs.*

DENNIS
I gave you my best! You're gettin' less from here on out.

STEVENS
(cheerful laugh)
A talented young buck like you has plenty in the tank! Back to ones everybody!

He exits.

STEVENS *(offstage)*
And…ACTION!

DENNIS
Jesus! You gotta be so loud? We're trying to have/a moment!

ROCK
We're in the scene!

STEVENS *(offstage)*
All right, scrapping that, resetting and ACTION!

Rock starts before Dennis can make trouble.

ROCK *(in character)*
(drunken slurring)
You oughta take responsibility for your country, son! There's a war on! Be a damn patriot!

DENNIS *(in character)*
There's other ways to help my country, Dad. And I'll be doing my part the best way I know how.

ROCK *(in character)*
You ungrateful son of a – this isn't how I raised you!

DENNIS *(in character)*
You raised me to never be a follower, Dad/and I –

STEVENS *(offstage)*
Cut!

DENNIS
(explosive distress)

Come on!

Stevens enters.

DENNIS

We're having a moment! You have any idea how *damaging* it is, blowing up a real moment?

ROCK

Speak for yourself. I'm happy doing my job.

DENNIS

Kiss-ass.

Rock is taken aback.

STEVENS

I'm trying to *help* you create a moment, Dennis. I've been doing this a lot longer/than you.

DENNIS

Doing what? It's a new goddamn age, buddy. We're not your robots, we're *artists!*

Stevens is shocked, on the verge of snapping.

ROCK
(peering beyond the audience)

What is —

STEVENS
(annoyed)

Yes? Do you have a contribution to the dialectic, Rock?

Rock points off beyond the audience.

ROCK

Do you think that was in the shot?

STEVENS

Was what in the shot?

He looks, and his mouth falls open.

STEVENS
(maintaining his calm)
Could we get somebody to please remove the god damn –
(temper rising)
red convertible from my GOD DAMN SHOT?

Liz enters and peers into the distance.

LIZ

Out in the pasture? Oh my goodness, that *is* a car. What in the
world?

STEVENS
(rage rising)
Does anybody have a sense of how and when this might have
happened?

DENNIS

Gosh, since we all gotta be here bright and early no matter what,
whoever did must'a been in a rush.

Stevens puts his face in his hands.

STEVENS

Is he here yet?

Dean jogs on.

DEAN

Sorry, ran a little bit late. Parked in the only spot I could find, hope
it's no bother.

                    STEVENS
I know what your game is, James. Bring your keys to a production
assistant, we'll get back to work.

                    DEAN
Ah, I sure am sorry, I went and dropped my keys somewhere along
the way.

            Stevens shakes his head, fuming.

                    ROCK
If you're going to let loose, we should move inside. There must be
fifteen hundred observers today.

                    STEVENS
I'm fine, Rock. Thank you.

            Dennis laughs.

                    STEVENS
Does something strike you as funny, Dennis?

                    DENNIS
Just wondering if this is harder or easier than filming a world war.

            *Stevens takes a sharp breath, then
            turns to Dennis.*

                    STEVENS
Come here please.

                    DENNIS
Nah, we should be getting back/to work.

                    STEVENS
COME HERE.

            *He catches his emotions. Dennis
            slouches over to him.*

STEVENS

Out of curiosity, what do you remember about the last week of April in 1945?

DENNIS

(laughs, unsure)

Not much, I was about nine.

STEVENS

As I imagined. Well, that was the week I visited Hell.

Dennis snorts.

ROCK

Oh come/on, you little –

STEVENS

It's all right. I don't tend to discuss that time, but in this case, I will make an exception. The last week of April in 1945, my crew and I accompanied the allies to a prison camp called Dachau. First, we passed boxcars filled with human bodies. Most were dead. With the shaved heads and the starvation, you couldn't tell how old they were, whether they were men or women. They were just –

(pause)

I picked up my camera, and I began to gather evidence. I went to film a woodpile, but –

(pause)

the woodpile was people. My men put down their cameras, they became nurses, they became ministers, but I filmed. For days. I didn't stop to sleep. There was too much to gather. My entire life had prepared me to arrive on this spot. This was my destiny.

He pauses, considering. Nobody moves.

STEVENS

With every blink, I left another small part of my humanity behind. I knew they wouldn't use it in the newsreels, but I was filming *evidence*. After my men were allowed to go home, I stayed for weeks, filling canisters with pain and cruelty. I had a family, I could have been with my son, but –

STEVENS (cont'd)
(pause)
And when they pried me away, I went home to prepare the footage.
And does anyone know what happened then?

ROCK
(small voice)
They used it in the trials.

STEVENS
They brought the films to Nuremberg, and they showed it as
evidence. This waterfall of gleeful sadism, bodies being moved by
bulldozers, shoved over cliffs to make room for more –
(voice finally breaking)
room for more *bodies*. And they made those…*creatures* sit in a
courtroom surrounded by human beings and they watched it all.

He takes a moment.

STEVENS
Then I had a choice. I could drink myself to death, or I could go
back to creating entertainment. Which leads me, ten years later, to
Texas, where I am making a pleasant diversion to help America
believe, for a few hours, that this world is worth living in. And two
little boys decided to play a trick on me. They inconvenienced me,
they wasted the time and money of quite a lot of people, because
these little boys thought I needed to learn to respect their power. But
I have seen flies on the drying eyeballs of living humans more
powerful than the two little boys who tried to bother me today.

He pauses, and then his mood
transforms.

STEVENS
(chipper and bright)
What a relaxing break we've all had! Now let's go find the keys to
that car and get back to work.

128

He turns, then whips back around and grabs Dennis by the shirt. He pulls Dennis' face to his.

STEVENS
(clenched teeth, enraged)
Is that all right with you, Dennis?

He shoves Dennis away. Dennis looks to Dean.

DENNIS
It wasn't just me.

Dean turns away.

STEVENS
Learn to take ownership, Dennis. Fan out, everyone, look for the keys, and let's find someone to tow that car if we can't find them. All right? Back to work please, daylight's wasting.

He exits. Dennis looks to Dean.

DENNIS
You hung me out to dry!

Dean won't look at Dennis, he just hurries offstage.

DENNIS
(shouting at Dean as he exits)
YOU SON OF A BITCH!

Rock and Liz exit.

DENNIS
(to audience)
And then I was alone again! Just like every day of my goddamn life, surrounded by idiots but alone!

DENNIS (cont'd)
(suddenly on a phone call)
Hello? You there or not, Ma? You not even gonna interrupt me this time? You must be in some kinda...oh THERE she is! Mother dearest, how ARE you this fine...Yeah? Ha! I bet you are!
(he listens a moment; his anger falters)
Look, what's going on, Ma? You not feeling all right?...Oh, ahright. Yeah...Because I wanted to – I don't know, talk to someone I guess. Not tryin' to be difficult... Fine. Can I – You still there? Ma?

He looks around, at a loss.

Dean enters and sits on the ground in the middle of the stage. Dennis exits. Dean draws his knees to his chest and puts his head on them.

Liz enters.

LIZ
Hello.

Dean looks up at her.

DEAN
Hello.

LIZ
You looked...quite struck earlier.

DEAN
Nobody ever talked to me like that.

LIZ
Nobody's ever scolded you?

Dean shakes his head. He's very upset.

LIZ
Nobody ever talked you like what?

*She sits next to him. Dean takes a
deep breath.*

DEAN
Like a man.

LIZ
Do you mean…I'm sorry, but – do you mean like a father?

Dean doesn't respond.

LIZ
You look very lonely.

Dean nods.

LIZ
You look a bit scared.

DEAN
(small voice)
I'm emptying faster than I can fill back up. When I get empty, I
drive. But I can't drive. And I'm emptying fast.

LIZ
You're frightened of…what, disappearing?

Dean shakes his head, near tears.

DEAN
I don't even know!

*Liz puts a hand on his thigh, it might
be sensual, but he puts his head on her
shoulder.*

LIZ
(smile)
Oh don't be so forthright, someone might see.

                         DEAN
Nobody's here.

                          LIZ
Well, I am a married woman. And a mother.

                         DEAN
I know. That's why.

                          LIZ
What is?

                         DEAN
I can't.

                          LIZ
Because I'm a mother?

            Dean shuts his eyes.

                         DEAN
Can I just sit like this a while? Is that OK?

            *Liz is shocked. And then she puts her
            arm around Dean's shoulder. He
            snuggles close.*

                          LIZ
Of course, my darling. Of course.

            He starts to shiver.

                          LIZ
            (singing quietly)
You are my sunshine, my only sunshine.
You make me happy when skies are gray.
You'll never know dear how much I love you.
Please don't take my sunshine away.

Dean lies down, putting his head in her
lap. She strokes his hair. The figments
enter and line up, sitting on the edge of
the stage, and give their news to the
audience in tired, depressed tones. Liz
and Dean stay onstage, Liz humming
You Are My Sunshine.

FIGMENT B

Blood-bath uprisings broke out in North Africa today. The death toll rose to 776.

FIGMENT E

Tomorrow, communists will return the body of an army captain whole plane was shot down by the Reds near the neutral zone last week.

FIGMENT D

A returning group of dignitaries reports that Russian farmers have only the necessities of life.

FIGMENT A

The Sudan may be on the brink of a civil war between the Muslim north and the Pagan south. An uprising among southern troops is gaining momentum.

FIGMENT E

The Soviet Union has offered to release four Danes held as prisoners since the second World War.

FIGMENT D

Secretary of State John Foster Dulles checked some of the rampant optimism growing out of the Geneva conference with Russia.

FIGMENT B

In a transmission to Congress, President Eisenhower today said that the free world, as a whole, is in a better position than ever before.

The figments are tired. They exit.

LIZ
(singing quietly)
You told me once, dear, you really loved me.
And nothing else could come between.
But now you've left me all by my lonesome.
You have shattered all of my dreams.

> *Dean takes a deep breath, holds it, and
> lets it out.*

> *Dennis enters.*

DENNIS
The rest of the time in Texas was all about survival. I didn't talk to a
single soul if I didn't have to. Acting's supposed to be what makes
me feel good, now it just felt like wasting time. I didn't see much of
Dean. I heard he spent a lotta time hunting jackrabbits.

> *Dean exits. Liz watches him go.*

DENNIS
When we finished the exteriors, we went back to LA to do the
interiors on the soundstage.

> *Liz stands. Stevens and Rock enter.*

DENNIS
And on that first day, when we all showed up at the studio, because
we all had to show up every day…well, not everybody did show up.

> *Stevens looks at his watch, sighs, and
> rubs his face.*

STEVENS
There's nothing to be done without him.

ROCK
(rueful chuckle)
Must be pretty liberating, not giving a rat's ass about anyone else.

LIZ

Rocky, have a little compassion.

ROCK

For an arrogant twit who thinks our workplace is his playground?

LIZ

Rock. You are too young to be this old.

STEVENS

Does anyone have a *clue* where he might be? I can shoot cutaways for an hour if you search.

Nobody speaks. Liz goes to Dennis.

LIZ

You must have some guess.

DENNIS

Even if I found him, I couldn't get him to listen.

LIZ

I'll go with you.

Dennis considers, then nods.

LIZ

(to Stevens)
A search party is mobilizing, Mr. Stevens.

STEVENS

Please don't lollygag.

*Stevens and rock exit. Dennis and Liz
go upstage.*

LIZ

Why here?

DENNIS

He told me about how the tar was made of animals that got trapped and stripped apart. He seemed miserable about it, but he's the kinda guy who likes being miserable, y'know?

Liz laughs.

DENNIS

Am I wrong?

LIZ

No. But I don't think you're right, either.

DENNIS

That's confusing.

LIZ

Well, so is life. Best to get used to it.

DENNIS

I thought you had life pretty much figured out.

LIZ

It takes years of careful practice to make it look that way.

DENNIS

I can't do it on my own.

LIZ

You don't have to. If you walk onto the Warners lot tomorrow and say, *I want to be a star, and I need help,* you'll have an army of support. They're your family.

DENNIS

But wouldn't that just make me…the same as everyone?

LIZ

Am I the same as everyone? Is Rock?

DENNIS

But I'm not Rock.

LIZ

He wasn't always Rock. He was Roy, the mechanic's son who never got cast in the school play.

Dennis considers

DENNIS

Are you happy?

LIZ

Some days.

DENNIS

I wanna be happy every day.

LIZ

(sigh)
Don't we all. You know, the tar may be animal bones, but ancient Indians used it to build boats. And those boats let them travel to the Channel Islands, fifty miles. They had no business traveling that far. But they did. Because of this tar. You don't have to see the dire part of *everything*.

Dennis thinks on that.

LIZ

Well, we were told not to lollygag.

She starts off.

DENNIS

Hey, if I *did* go talk to someone…say I needed help…who would I go talk to?

LIZ

Anyone. That's the wonderful thing about having a family. Where else should we search?

DENNIS

He never invited me anyplace else. I don't even know where he lives.

Liz nods and exits.

DENNIS

(to audience)
He didn't show up the rest of the day. Stevens sent us home early.
And so…yeah, I did it again. I didn't think it'd work, and maybe that
was self-fulfilling. But I had to try. I had to –
(slightly away, talking on the phone)
ask her to meet me, please. I know…I know! Just – I have something
to say. I've been doing so much thinking. I need – please, I know!
Just ask her! Googie's in an hour! Hello?
(to audience)
And when I got down there –

*Dennis goes to a booth. Bobby enters
and sits across from him. Dennis is
surprised to see him.*

BOBBY

She's not coming. You have to stop.

DENNIS

I know I screwed up, can't we pretend it was practice? I was drunk, I
was confused but/it's all –

BOBBY

We always think we've got it figured out *now*, right? We always think,
I was an idiot a year ago, but now I got it together. Then another year later,
Nah, I was an idiot THEN, now I finally got it together.

DENNIS

Can you give her a message? I could write something/down.

BOBBY

What's your game, Dennis? She's got better guys than you crawling
all over her. Why would you be special?

DENNIS

She said I made her feel safe.

BOBBY

(dry bitter laugh)

Well thanks for the help.

DENNIS

It was one dumb, drunk phone call!

BOBBY

You don't know what you don't know. Try and learn that.

DENNIS

Hey, you know you're younger than me, right? Little prick!

BOBBY

(standing up)

She moved out, by the way, so don't bother her mom again. Feel free to keep trying to see her, but it's me who'll keep showing up, and I don't think we'll have a good time.

DENNIS

Wait! What don't I know?

BOBBY

There are other pretty girls, Dennis.

DENNIS

It's not about pretty!

Bobby exits. Dennis puts his face on the table.

DENNIS

It's about SOMEBODY being glad I'm alive!

He slouches out of the booth and exits.

> *Stevens enters, and gazes out into the*
> *audience, lost in painful contemplation.*
> *Dean enters upstage, quiet.*

DEAN

Hey. Mr. Stevens.

> *Stevens startles, and turns to see Dean.*
> *He chuckles.*

STEVENS

You're a bit late.

DEAN

Everyone went home?

STEVENS

Did you expect them to wait all night?

DEAN

No.

STEVENS

You may as well go, too. I can't fire you, I'm resigned to just hoping the dailies make them happy enough not to care I'm behind schedule and over budget. Again.

DEAN

I missed a day because I needed the day. Next time you make me waste a day, I'm taking two. That ain't a threat, it's just a promise. Time after that, I'm taking three.

STEVENS

I can't imagine you believe this is good for your future.

DEAN

I don't have a future if I don't take care of myself. Y'know when people do something hard, and they say, *That really took it outta me?*

> *Stevens nods.*

DEAN

I'm not kidding when I say it. I make myself *hurt*, cuz it's the only way to make myself good. But I gotta keep some kinda balance or…it ends bad for me.

STEVENS

What do you mean you hurt?

DEAN

I don't eat, I don't sleep, I just *work!* I can't do it like other people! This is how I do it! And I'm just trying to stay alive! I'm tired! I'm emptying out!

STEVENS

All right! All right.

DEAN

I came here to ask for help!

STEVENS

I said it on day one, I can't make the exceptions for you that other/directors –

DEAN

I want direction! I'll listen! I never did anything like this. I made normal pictures. This one's…so *big*. I need help or I – I won't have anything left in me to find.

STEVENS

Are you saying you want to work on your scenes after hours?

DEAN

I'm ready to learn. Do you have time?

STEVENS

Let's talk in the morning, we'll find a/time to –

DEAN

Do you have time now?

Stevens is caught off guard. He considers.

DEAN
(nakedly vulnerable)

I need help.

STEVENS

Yes, all right. Come here. Let's work together.

He holds out his arm, and Dean goes to him. They exit, talking quietly.

Dennis enters, pacing and furious.

DENNIS
(to audience, angry)

I didn't talk to anyone for two days.

Figment E enters and walks close to Dennis.

FIGMENT E

The earth is approximately four thousand million years old.

Dennis tries to ignore Figment E

DENNIS

I hardly slept!

Figment D enters and stands close to Dennis.

FIGMENT D

But at that time, the Earth's rotation was much faster, so days were as short as ten hours!

Figments B and C enter.

DENNIS

I was ready to *finally* be part of/something!

FIGMENT B

A day on Venus is 120 Earth hours!

Figment A enters.

FIGMENT C

But it was originally the same length as our days.

ENSEMLE A

How do we explain this slowing planetary rotation?

DENNIS

(getting frantic)

So where did it get me?

FIGMENT A

Jupiter has a mass two and a half times the rest of the planets *combined!*

FIGMENT E

But there could be a hundred million planetary systems similar to our own!

DENNIS

I was alone when I was angry! And I was alone when I tried to be something! Alone in/the universe!

FIGMENT B

Jupiter is five hundred million miles from the sun!

FIGMENT C

The sun is a hundred and fifty quadrillion miles from the center of the galaxy!

DENNIS

What was it gonna TAKE?

FIGMENT A

Our galaxy has satellite star systems that move around our galaxy!

FIGMENT A

Their rotation takes two million years!

Dennis is frightened and overwhelmed.
He covers his ears and tries to evade the
figments, but they circle around him.

FIGMENT D

Outside our galaxy, there are *other* galaxies!

FIGMENT D

One has been measured at ten quintillion miles away!

The figments tighten on Dennis.

FIGMENT E

It's likely there are galaxies as far away as ten million parsecs!

FIGMENT B

And a parsec is eighteen trillion miles!

FIGMENT C

That's eighteen trillion times ten million!

The figments have now completely
swallowed Dennis, becoming something
like a rugby scrum.

FIGMENT A

That's —

Dennis howls and the figments explode
away. Dean enters and Dennis spins to
face him.

DENNIS

YOU!

Dean watches from a distance. The
figments clear.

DENNIS

You said if you were gonna hand me a gun, you were gonna teach me
to use it! And what did you do? Just twist my head and use me and
throw me away and for WHAT? What was the POINT?

Dean saunters closer.

DENNIS

Huh? Come on! For once in your damn life, TALK TO ME! I hated
you, then I worshipped you – yeah, I did! And you KNEW it! So
don't you think you OWE me a little DECENCY? You got a
RESPONSIBILITY to people in this world! Use your BRAIN! Take
OWNERSHIP!

Dean chuckles.

DENNIS

GODDAMN IT, COME ON!

Dennis slips into character, and a
scene, without seeming to notice.

DENNIS *(in character)*

Let's go! You been askin' for this a long damn time!
(puts up his fists)
I'm gonna knock your goddamn head off for what you done to me!

Dean chuckles, spits at the ground and
turns away.

DENNIS *(in character)*
(savage)

You son of a BITCH! Don't you DARE walk away from me! We
been through too much! I won't stand for it! You get back here and
FACE ME!

                    DEAN *(in character)*
                (turning back)
You're not worth the effort.

                Dennis roars with rage.

                    STEVENS
And cut!

                Dennis looks around. He's heaving
                with breath, dazed and awed. The
                world looks new.

                    DENNIS
Where was I?

                    DEAN
In a real moment.
                (he claps Dennis on the arm)
Congratulations, Dennis. Been a long trip, huh?

                He exits.

                    STEVENS
Very good work, Dennis. Thank you.

                Stevens exits, too. Dennis looks around
                like he's just awoken from a nightmare.

                    DENNIS
                (whispered)
Wow.

                He clears his throat. He's hoarse.

                    DENNIS
Just one minute. Please.

                Mary enters, and crosses her arms.

DENNIS

I know I shouldn't be here. And this really will be the last time. I didn't agree last time, but now I'm volunteering. If you make me leave, I'll leave and that'll be it. I promise.

MARY

Then leave.

DENNIS

(sigh)

OK.

Natalie enters, just barely.

NATALIE

It's all right, Mary. I'll talk to him.

MARY

No!

NATALIE

I want to. Let's just sit right here, Dennis.

MARY

I'm watching from the window. If this girl starts crying, I'm grabbing a butcher's knife.

Dennis holds up his hands in
agreement. Natalie goes to the edge of
the stage and sits. Dennis goes and sits,
too. For a moment, they're quiet.

NATALIE

Are you going to say anything?

DENNIS

I'm just enjoying a moment of you actually wanting to talk to me.

NATALIE

Willing to.

DENNIS

Sure.

Beat.

DENNIS

I thought I could use you to make me better. Then I thought I could force you to think I'm better, and that'd make it true. But really – I felt seen by you. As long as we're talkin' now, I feel seen. That means a lot. I see you, too. I didn't always act like it. Wasn't always true, I guess. It's true now.

NATALIE

I'm glad.

DENNIS

So I don't want to be your curse. But I'm done trying to force things to be a certain way.
(pause)
The work felt good today. I think I have a sense of how to keep it that way. But when I was done, I wanted to share it with you. Not because I wanna be your man, I know that's not happening. But this world's hard enough, and sharing things used to make it a little easier for me. What about you?

Natalie nods. She's close to crying.

DENNIS

Ah Hell, I stepped in it again.

NATALIE

I'm just remembering how a few months ago the world seemed so much simpler than it does now.

DENNIS

Is it Nick?

Natalie laughs and wipes her face.

NATALIE

Nick's a child. You know he forgot to write into his contract that he'd be paid for postproduction?

DENNIS

(huge laugh)

What?

NATALIE

Almost like it was never about the work at all. He just wanted...

Beat.

DENNIS

So your mom was OK with you moving in with Mary?

NATALIE

She'll have to be. Or I'll make a strong case for reckless endangerment.

DENNIS

What happened?

Natalie considers, then holds out her wrist.

NATALIE

You see that scar?

DENNIS

Oh my god, how'd I never notice that?

NATALIE

You were never looking.

DENNIS

It's awful.

NATALIE

When I was a little girl, she made me do a stunt for some stupid kids'

NATALIE (cont'd)

picture. The bridge I had to cross wasn't safe. And I knew it wasn't. But she said I was paranoid. And I believed her. So I fell.

DENNIS

You'd still hold her accountable for that? You think that'd hold up?

NATALIE

No, but that's the curse. It's been happening again and again for ten years. It happened right after you left, after we wrapped. I was supposed to meet with a particular star. One of my favorites.
                    (small sad chuckle)
He wanted to talk about a project. He asked to meet in his hotel room. And it didn't feel right. But my mother said it was typical, it was what they do in this business. And I DID want to meet him.

DENNIS

          (urgent)

Who was it?

NATALIE

He told me he'd ruin my life if I told anyone what we did.

Her breath hitches.

DENNIS

          (savage)
You mean what HE did.

Natalie nods.

DENNIS

You gotta tell me who it is. I'll murder him. I don't care.

NATALIE

You can't Dennis.

DENNIS

I'll find a way!

NATALIE

It happened. I just have to figure out how to keep going.
(huge breath)
I've been wanting to tell you. I knew you'd be the right kind of angry.

DENNIS

I'm glad you did.

NATALIE

We can't start fresh. The world doesn't work like that. But we can start again. Googie's some night?

DENNIS

Sounds great.

NATALIE

I'll have my people call your people.

She hugs his shoulders, then stands.

NATALIE

It's so much colder than it looks, isn't it?

She exits. Dennis looks off, considering.

Rock enters.

ROCK *(in character)*

You have to forget what happened, son. You can't change it.

Dennis jumps up.

DENNIS *(in character)*

I'm not forgettin' a damn thing! I'm carryin' it the rest'a my days!

Rock goes to him and grabs his elbow.

ROCK *(in character)*

You can be strong without being wild. You know that, don't you?

Dennis grits his teeth, then sighs.

> DENNIS *(in character)*

All right.

> ROCK *(in character)*

You always were a willful boy. I thought you'd grow out of it. Now the best I can hope is you grow *into* it. You know, son, there's something called polite society. You need to learn to live/within it.

> DENNIS *(in character)*

If I don't like the way they world is, I'll change the world! Cause the world ain't changin' me!

> STEVENS *(offstage)*

Cut.

Rock and Dennis drop character.
Dennis is satisfied, at peace. Stevens
enters.

> STEVENS

Very good work, everyone. That's a wrap for tonight. We're almost finished.

> DENNIS

Hey, Mr. Stevens. You haven't heard anything from Dean have you?

> STEVENS

James finished his commitment. He's free to do as he likes until the premiere.

> DENNIS

But it's been a couple weeks, I just hoped maybe you heard somethin'.

Dean enters behind Dennis. He's
dressed in turtleneck and glasses again.

DEAN

What kinda somethin' did you hope for?

Rock sees Dean, shakes his hand grudgingly, then exits.

DENNIS

How long you been standin' there?

DEAN

Long enough.

STEVENS

Good to see you, James. Will you be around?

DEAN

I might. Good t'see you, too.

Stevens nods, and exits.

DENNIS

So where you been?

DEAN

I took a drive.

DENNIS

For two weeks?

DEAN

And I'm not done yet. You wanna go down to Googie's, grab somethin' to eat?

DENNIS

Really? Yeah!

They go to the booth and sit.

DEAN

I been reading this book by Mark Twain, *The Mysterious Stranger*. You read it?

DENNIS

Never heard of it.

DEAN

Well he never finished it. Worked and worked, put *years* in, but it never felt right.

DENNIS

Sounds exhausting.

DEAN

It's about this young guy, or he looks young. He's older than he looks. And he comes to this town, and he can see the future. He can tell what's gonna happen, who's gonna die. The townsfolk beg him to prevent it. Prevent that pain. So he tries, but…

He gets out a pack of cigarettes and empties it onto the table.

DEAN

He just makes everything worse.

He starts moving the cigarettes around.

DEAN

What was he supposed to do, y'know? They asked. He tried. But the moral of the story, at the end, is – the world around you isn't real. It's a dream. The only thing that really exists is you. And all *you* are is a thought in your head.

DENNIS

I never knew you liked to read.

DEAN

I'm contracted for nine pictures in the next six years. I been thinking how to play it.

He separates eight cigarettes into four pairs.

DEAN

I do four more years like this, back to back pictures. Still one more picture to squeeze in somewhere.

He sits back, exhausted.

DENNIS

By then you'll have a whole shelf full'a Oscars before you're even 30, you'll be able to negotiate however you want, this town'll be over a barrel for you.

DEAN

(defeated)
Four more years like this.

DENNIS

I know it was hard, but I had some good times. Knowing I'm getting better makes it worth it.

DEAN

You don't feel yourself emptying yet?

DENNIS

Nah. Guess I'm not as good as you yet!

DEAN

You don't want this life, Dennis.

DENNIS

I do.

DEAN

Then I hope you find another way to get it. Because the harder I work the faster I disappear. Sooner or later, I'll be so far gone there's no comin' back.

DENNIS

You're still here.

DEAN

You're pretty optimistic. Maybe you're the new model. When I saw you acting back there today with Rock…I think you might be. Dennis –

> *He reaches across the table and grabs Dennis' hand.*

DEAN

You were *great*.

> *Dennis' eyes well up. Dean chuckles.*

DEAN

Glad it means somethin' to ya. But a real actor never cries unless he's in character.

> *He stands up.*

DENNIS

You're going?

DEAN

Gotta rest up. I'm headed to Salinas for a race. Then I'll get to *really* drive. I need it. The faster I go, the more I feel the blood comin' back. After this year, I need to drive *fast*. Just move through space. Move through time. Just a human being. Just me.

> *He lights a cigarette.*

DENNIS

Good luck.

DEAN

Don't need it.

DENNIS

Hang on a second.

Dean waits.

DENNIS

It's fun though, isn't it? At least admit that. You can't do all this just to punish your mom for dying.

Dean smokes and thinks.

DEAN

Five years ago, I was at UCLA, they cast me in *Hamlet,* I was Laertes. Biggest thrill of my entire life, to this day.

He relaxes as he talks, starts to smile.

DEAN

I felt like I was in a dream. I wasn't thinking about a million things, I wasn't thinking at all. Just *being.* Just a nice, simple reality. People go their whole lives hoping for that. And y'know what? Review in the student paper was *terrible.* They said, *James Dean is a name to forget.*

He and Dennis laugh.

DEAN

See ya further on down the road, Dennis.

He walks upstage

DENNIS

I figured maybe that's the turning point.

Dennis exits.

*The figments enter and gather behind
Dean, and he falls back into their*

*arms. The figments become a car—or
something like the spirit of speed—
carrying Dean along. He's weightless,
lost in the rush, euphoric and
intoxicated, refueling.*

*As the figments move, their motion
becomes more scattered, less
harmonious. The crash has begun.*

*Dean dies. The figments lower him and
carry him offstage.*

Dennis reenters.

DENNIS
(to audience)
So I figure maybe now we're friends. Real friends.

He sighs. The next part is hard.

DENNIS
But then I was at home, and –

*There's a knock at the door. Behind
Dennis, the figments and Dean exit.*

DENNIS
It's open!

Natalie enters, distraught.

DENNIS
Hey, what's shakin'?

NATALIE
Nick called me.

DENNIS
What'd he do this time?

NATALIE

Dennis, I need you to promise you'll stay calm. All right?

Dennis goes very still.

DENNIS

What did he say?

NATALIE

James Dean is dead.

DENNIS
(impulsive, screaming)
YOU'RE A LIAR!

*He grabs her, violent and manic. She
screams and recoils, and he releases her.
Both are shocked, but her face quickly
turns to cold anger. It's over. She exits.
Dennis breaths very heavily, shaking.*

DENNIS
(to audience)
And the next day it was all anyone talked about. How he couldn't
wait to get to Salinas before he opened the car up. Really see if he
could break the speedometer. Everyone thought he was just showin'
off. But everyone thought a lotta things. Nobody really knew.
(angry pause)
That was just supposed to be the *beginning!* So I decided I'd carry it
on. Be the new model.

*The figments enter and stand around
him, observing.*

DENNIS

I was just trying to do what he taught me! If that meant showing up
to set drunk, telling a director –
(whirling on the figments)
When I run this town, lotta heads are gonna roll, baby! I'll have you

DENNIS (cont'd)

all in chains!

(shakes head)

I was just doing like he taught me. So I took it too far. I drank, I doped – I was difficult! Like you always said. I couldn't be directed. I fell off the edge.

He looks to the figments for support.
They silently judge him.

DENNIS

(to audience)

I know, I was difficult! I just said it! You happy now, Ma? You win. The prophecy comes true, congrats. But if I'm difficult, if I'm the guy who's so DIFFICULT that Warners tears up his contract and burns it, then you MADE me this way! So I thought you'd wanna know how it happened, how I LOST the one good thing that ever happened. I learned to be great, and in the bargain I learned I was difficult. I accept it! Hey, I'm almost done! One more minute! Because that's where we are now. But I'm still goin'. Here's your little epilogue. All right?

He holds out his hands for agreement,
then nods.

DENNIS

I drove out here to tell you all'a this, and then who knows what I was gonna do. Maybe I was gonna put a gun in my mouth, I don't know, I never knew. I never did learn to use my brain.

Deep breath.

DENNIS

But on my way here, I was comin' down the hill outside town, and just as I go over the crest, my brakes give out. And then I'm just...*flying*. Faster and faster like my wings were on fire. I've never moved so fast. And I realize this is it. I won't even live as long as he did. And what did I achieve?

Another deep breath.

DENNIS

And then my eyes go to the rearview.

The figments move apart, and Dean is
onstage, partially obscured by shadow,
as in the opening.

DENNIS

And he's there. In the back, arm up, the picture of relaxation. And he
says —

DEAN

It's OK, Dennis. There's an emergency brake.

Beat.

DENNIS

And he was right. So I pulled it.

Dean exits, along with the figments.

DENNIS

It took a little while, and I didn't know if it'd work, but soon enough
I slowed down, and then…it wasn't too late. I still had time after all.
So I looked back —

He turns around. Everyone is gone. He
turns back.

DENNIS

And now — I guess I just wanted to help you understand. Because
then maybe you could help *me* understand. So — please. I don't know
where the brake is. And Ma…I feel *so empty.*

END OF PLAY.

Made in the USA
Monee, IL
30 December 2022

24131981R00094